Caught Between Two Worlds

Marion Weatherburn

CHAMPION MEDIA
Adelaide

Published by Champion Digital Media

Copyright © 2016 Marion Weatherburn

www.psychiclikenoother.com.au

All rights reserved. This book or any portion thereof may not be reproduced or used in any manner whatsoever without the express written permission of the publisher except for the use of brief quotations in a book review.

2nd Edition
First printed November 2016
This edition printed January 2017

ISBN 978-0-646-96383-9

www.championmedia.com.au

Caught Between Two Worlds

For Nairina and Jennifer
Just because I love you...

By writing this book, I hope to touch your Soul, even without you knowing perhaps. I hope to set your feet firmly on this beautiful Spiritual Path we call life. Whilst I have made a very dear sacrifice in writing these words, I hope you do not have to ever experience the pain of being "Caught Between Two Worlds".

My deep love goes out to each and everyone of you whose Soul chooses to read my book. Most of the words of guidance are not my own, but those of my Team.

Whilst I ask you to pay attention to the words, it is the gaps in between the words that are most important, because that is where I have placed my love for me, you and life.
That's how much love I have to give.

Marion Weatherburn, 2016

Table Of Contents

Foreword	1
Acknowledgements	5
Introduction	9
PART ONE: Experience	
Discovering My Gift	19
Making Sense of My Gift	41
PART TWO: Readings	
What A Reading Can and Can't Tell You	53
James: A Child in Turmoil	57
Annie: A Desperate Mum's Plea	70
Renee: To Read or Not To Read	79
Sophie: Secret Lover Surprise	86
Heather: How Do You Know You're Dead	92
Cazz: Pennies From Heaven	95

Helen: Silence Is Golden	100
Ted: Pyschic Testing Underway	104
Every Day is Mother's Day	109
Evelyn & Emma: A Special Bond	113
Lauren: Who You Gonna Call?	120
Kimberly: The Woman in the Mirror	123
Lexi: Boyfriends and Kangaroos	135
Sharon: The L Word	138
Leslie: A Friend Taken Too Soon	141
Uncle George and His Girls	144
Chloe: Children as Teachers	150
Sheridan: Elders in the Garden	157
Diane: Seeking Justice	161
Murni: An Empty Seat at the Bar	165
John: Fright Night	174
Stu: A Happy Sceptic	178
Riley: Triple N	181
Six Beautiful Vietnamese	191
June: Geraldton in Wartime	195
A Collection of Short Stories	202

PART THREE: Advice

Soul Food	221
Life's Little Secrets	238

Foreword

Marion has a very warm and caring nature that is driven by her desire to help others and make a difference in the world. The warmth and empathy that Marion conducts herself with during her readings is characteristic of the beautiful and caring person she truly is.

I have seen firsthand the emotional connection Marion has with each and every story that she shares throughout her book. She talks about the people that have come to her with such passion and heartfelt commitment. From my own experience, the very moment I met Marion I felt an instant friendship. It was as if I had known her my whole life. Still to this day Marion is genuinely interested in how things are going and is the first person to offer help whenever she can. Our reading was the beginning of a true friendship.

Each story in this book is very close to Marion's heart and just like the people she has been able to help through her gentle words and insight, Marion too has been touched

FOREWORD

by those same people and feels compelled to share these gifts with her readers.

She has specifically chosen each story carefully for the heartfelt and inspirational message that they can bring to the reader. Messages of hope, closure, inspiration and love.

Just as a teacher can learn from their students or a parent learns from their children, the growth of knowledge is universal. Age is not a factor. We are continually on a cycle of growth in terms of knowledge and understanding and we gain the most when we open our mind, heart and soul, allowing ourselves to be truly touched by the experiences of others. It is only then that we can fully appreciate and see the lessons put in front of us as building blocks for personal growth and seize the opportunities presented to us. In the darkest depths of despair there is always hope. An optimistic outlook is your strongest weapon for gaining fulfilment and peace. Through struggle comes success and the appreciation of its rewards. I believe this book can help you better understand this.

Understanding of where another has come from - their struggles, heartaches and strengths - also inspires us and gives us an insight into our own world in terms of challenging our prior beliefs. Our goal should be to grow as an individual through reflection and empathy for others.

Let the experiences presented in this book inspire you to not only deepen your understanding and empathy towards others but to let them assist you to also live a more fulfilled life. Focus on not only what lays before you but also to listen to your inner voice. Trust your instincts and let your inner child shine through. Sometimes our greatest achievements can only be gained by truly having faith in ourselves and taking a leap into the unknown. I wouldn't be where I am today had I not trusted my instincts and had faith in my own strength to escape what would have been inevitably a lifetime of control and heartache for myself and my children. Marion helped me to rediscover the strength that I had miss placed along my journey.

In my experience, true happiness can only be found by letting go of artificial and temporary fixes and taking the time to discover the basic forms of love and kindness that we are instinctively born with and so often lose along the way. The world is full of unknown and incredible miracles that we don't even notice because we are so focused on the material world.

Let this book help you to open your heart and soul to begin questioning the most important things in life and looking beyond the obvious to what our soul desires in order to be truly content.

Marion has touched the lives of those in her book, let her also touch the lives of all her readers. Learn and gain inspiration from the messages that have come from her incredible ability to connect with both the physical and spiritual beings.

Melissa Bennett, October 2016

Acknowledgements

Andy, you loved me unconditionally. You supported and encouraged me even though you didn't like or understand this work I do. Thank you for loving me enough to let me finish writing this book that will lead to more. You gave me the Gift of two beautiful children and the Gift of this book. Thank you for an amazing 27 years. I loved you and I miss you.

Jess, thank you for choosing me to be your Mum. You have taught me more than you will ever know. You taught me that there are other ways of looking at life that make just as much sense as the way I look at life. I am proud of the beautiful woman and mother you have become and love you unconditionally.

Kaleb, you were born with a smile on your face and your only job in this life seems to be to make people happy with that smile! I'm proud to be your "Glam-ma"!

Ryan, thank you for ringing me every day to make sure I am ok! Your phone calls kept me going when nothing

ACKNOWLEDGEMENTS

else could. Always listen to your heart Ryan, it will get you through the tough times. As my first born, you made me feel like I was unwrapping my favourite Christmas present every day. I still feel that way. I am proud of the man you have become and love you dearly.

Dad, I love you and I never thought I would say that, let alone put it in writing. I have been witness to the most amazing transformation of a person that I have ever seen in my lifetime. Your strength and love is what got me through the past 18 months and I will be forever grateful to have you back in my life. I am proud to call you my Dad.

Mum, I love you more every day. I admire your strength and will to live with all you've endured. Without you, I would not be writing this book. I am glad I picked you to be my Mum.

Nairina, we have shared so much in this life. Our highs and our lows have formed the glue that bonds us together. For life. I have watched and admired you over the years. Watched you struggle and admired you getting through. You inspire me. You accepted me into your life and your heart. I was the lucky one! Thank you for your unconditional love and friendship and the many times you passed me the tissues when I didn't have the strength to reach for them myself. You are family to me.

Jennifer, you are the sister I always yearned for. The most amazing of coincidences brought us together in the first place. The most amazing of unconditional love continues to keep us together. Even at my worst, you accepted, loved and hugged me. Jen, I want to thank you for liking me enough to love me. You and I have a connection no one can ever take away. We have shared so much more than I can fit into this paragraph so I will have to squeeze my love into the spaces between the words.

Matt C, you are one of a kind and will remain my friend for life. I admire your inner strength, wit and wisdom. You taught me that I really am ok, just as you are!

Karen R, you are the kind of woman I wanted to grow up to be. You believed in me when I didn't. Thank you for teaching me the very important difference between a golf ball and a watermelon. I still have that golf ball today!

Sharon A, my oldest and most gracious friend. We are connected by an invisible thread that keeps us connected despite the distance and the years. You were my inspiration.

Stuart P, I have been to hell and back and you were with me every step of the way. Thank you for accepting me as I am, weirdness and all. 36 years ago you asked me to marry you and I never answered you. Despite everything that has been thrown our way on the journey, I am so very glad you kept me alive and kicking! I have never in my life seen a man accept change for the better the way you have. You and I have learnt so much this past 18 months. I know that we will now benefit from that knowledge and connection that we have.

Marg, thank you for being there for my mum and dad when I wasn't. Thank you for being there for me, when I wasn't.

Josh, thank you for liking my book enough to edit it.

ACKNOWLEDGEMENTS

Despite your scepticism, you have been able to capture the essence of me exactly as I was hoping you would. I've read and re read this book hundreds of times over the past 16 years and only when I read your final manuscript did I actually realise how good it could be. You reignited my interest and made my book really interesting. Thank you.

And lastly, to my Team. Opa B; Opa D; Joop D; Mark and Staven. I look forward to thanking you in person for being by my side every step of every day, even when I chose to ignore you! Without you, I wouldn't have been able to help the hundreds of lives that I have. The love and gratitude I feel I cannot put into words as words are simply not enough.

To whomever it may concern that listened to me while I ranted, raved, cried throughout my life time ~ Thank you for everything and more!

Please note: *some names and places have been changed for privacy reasons.*

Introduction

When you picked up this book, what were you hoping for? Perhaps that an Australian Medium wrote this book intrigued you. Perhaps the testimonials from each of the people whose story I use in this book have given you confidence in the authenticity of the stories. Or, maybe you too feel that you are often caught between two worlds. Maybe you are looking for proof that there's more to life? Maybe you are a sceptic but secretly curious? Maybe this book is just the confirmation you need right now?

Perhaps you are intrigued by my being able to see and feel events that not all people can. One way or the other, learning about Psychics and Mediums well may raise questions for you about your own life. Maybe you are one of many who knows your loved ones are still around and you want to strengthen your connections with them. I invite you to join me on this adventure through my life so that you can better understand how the events in my life

INTRODUCTION

have shaped who I am.

I have done almost a thousand Readings. Of those, I now offer you the 20 or 30 most profound. All Readings are special, that's for sure. However, the others are about spiritual growth and direction for the person, along with some basic spiritual guidance and clarification about their own journeys.

For many people, having a Psychic Reading is about direction, clarification, information, healing and closure. I always recommend that those I read for expect the unexpected. My Reading for Sophie, which you will hear about later, taught me that we are all energy - whether alive in this life or the next life. She also explained to me that as Psychic Mediums we cannot just ring the doorbell upstairs above the clouds and summon forward the Soul of a person passed over simply because the person who has come for the Reading wants to make contact. That is just impossible.

All famous Psychic Mediums out there state vehemently that this is simply not possible. Be wary of anyone who claims they can do this. This would be like turning up at a stranger's house, ringing their doorbell and expecting them to be home and awaiting your arrival with a familiar handshake and a cup of tea. Again, it simply does not work this way.

Psychics understand that Spirits, whether alive in this life or the next, will come through in a Reading if they want to or if you need to hear a very important spiritual message. As I have been countless times, I believe you'll be pleasantly surprised as you read these stories.

Welcome to my heart, my life as it's been lived: caught between two worlds.

Within these pages, I plan to give you a glimpse of what it's like to be a Psychic. I'll also talk to you about how to stay connected to those who matter to you the most. I'll share my own childhood experience in order that young Psychics who have questions and doubts about their gifts may be reassured. I hope that my experiences will help show how a child with this gift might feel or view things.

I also hope it illustrates how we, as people who love the gifted young, can help them to understand and embrace their abilities. For each of us, figuring out our gifts in life is part of our journey to becoming enlightened human beings. My hope is that in reading the following, you may gain real insight into the life of a person with special abilities. I hope it will help you to better understand where Psychics and Mediums come from and what kinds of potential we have. Understanding the unknown is half the battle of expanding your spiritual beliefs.

It took me many years to realise that what I possess is a gift. For most of my life, it has just made me feel like a misfit. I've never understood those who envy me for it, as mostly I only envy those who don't have it. But I now feel it's important to term it as a gift.

I am a Psychic, and sometimes, a Medium. This means I can see future events, I can get into a person's mind and communicate with those passed over who wish to make contact. I cannot communicate with those passed over if

INTRODUCTION

they do not want to communicate or are not even aware that they can. I will go into more detail about this later in this book.

I have often wished that someone would come up with a better word than Psychic to describe people like me. What with all the wannabes, con artists, gypsies and witch stereotypes out there, the word has been forever tainted. That makes it difficult for those of us that are authentic.

I was born in 1962. A daughter of Dutch migrants to Australia. I'm now old enough to have accepted what I do and young enough still to question it, keeping me grounded. Even when I was little, I was not a typical kid. I always knew when someone was lying to me and this made it very hard for me to make friends. I was a loner and a misfit and I knew it.

As time went on, I learnt to trust the "inner voice" that I knew did not belong to me. What I worried about was being watched when I was doing something naughty like stealing chocolate from the local deli. Or, if I lied to my parents about where I was. My Opa was a very big part of my life at that age. When I was naughty, I feared that Opa would stop talking to me because his good advice was being wasted on me.

I have been through a lot more serious events in my life than those just mentioned. Events when I ignored my Guide, thinking it was my conscience giving me a hard time, which is sometimes called guilt. But, I am glad to say that even though I chose not to listen on occasion, my Opa is still guiding me, albeit in a different way.

CAUGHT BETWEEN TWO WORLDS

Opa is now a part of my Team, which is the term I use for my group of spiritual guides. I'll explain more about Guides later. Before I understood who they were and why they were there, I was always encouraged to do the right thing by my Team, and generally I ignored their guidance as I thought it was just my conscience and that there would be no consequence!

That was before I learnt about Karma.

After all, this was my human experience and maybe it really was just my imagination giving me a hard time.

I went to a Catholic primary school and loved questioning religion with the nuns. Where was the proof? I preferred to talk to heaven personally when I was by myself, usually walking around outside. I always felt very connected to a higher power and I was very sensitive to all energies around me.

I always silently suspected that God was not real but I would never say it aloud in case He was listening. Incidentally though, isn't it interesting that whenever someone needs help in their lives and they don't believe, they often still pray or ask for help from a divine source? Also, whenever someone hurts themselves, one of the first things that people say is "Oh God!" Why? Curiously, "Oh My God" or "OMG" has become a form of punctuation. A heavily overused form of punctuation in my opinion.

I have always believed in Angels, Jesus and Mother Mary. Oh, and miracles! Definitely miracles! I always wanted to believe in Heaven and God, because I wanted to be sure that there was indeed a place held for me when

INTRODUCTION

I passed through that golden gate.

Upon reflection, it was way back in high school when my Team first started to let me know they were around. It was through some amazing coincidences, too many to even list in this book, although I have shared some of the most special ones. They would show me impressions of people and events and give me premonitions. I never thought anything of it. I always found it extremely helpful to know about things before they happened, and it always amused me that I knew. I never questioned it. I thought everyone could see it. It seemed so normal. Even these days, I'm not sure I understand it all that much more. But that's ok. I came up with a saying years ago that "we keep learning until all our fingers are the same length".

I spent my years trying everything I could to feel normal and be like all the other girls in my school. I loved roller skating and sailing. It was the speed, freedom and exhilaration of my hair blowing in the wind. It made me feel normal. Yet, my favourite TV shows as a child were *Casper the Friendly Ghost* and *Bewitched*. I just loved Samantha on Bewitched and on a recent visit to Salem in the United States, had my photo taken with her memorial. So I knew there was something more to all this, but couldn't put a finger on it.

When the TV series *Touched by An Angel* first came out, I knew that everything I had been feeling or had felt was real. I identified with the main character, Monica, on a profound level. I was spellbound. I also never missed an episode of *The Ghost Whisperer*, a TV series based on all the Readings ever done by world famous Medium James Van Praagh. I loved watching the way Melinda worked. It was just like me. Again, I felt understood. At least, by the universe.

As I got older, I adored watching Alison DuBois in *Medium* and now have all of her books. While reading her autobiography I found many similarities between her and I. Alison gave me the courage to write my own story. This was the final confirmation that I was not alone in everything I had been experiencing but did not understand. There was nothing wrong with me at all. If anything, I was starting to realise that I had a Gift.

I felt understood, and a huge burden finally left me.

I felt like I'd come home.

Since then, I've undergone a huge transformation, resulting in an acceptance of my Gift. However, I still have to live in the physical world and I still feel caught between two worlds. Thus, my decision to share my experience in the pages of this book. May it inspire you, as the events recounted within have inspired me.

PART ONE:
Experience

Discovering My Gift

The Clear Voice On The Cliff

I was at my end. It was April 1986 and I had driven to the edge of a cliff on the Murray River. Not to drive off it, just to find answers and withdraw from the painful world that had been my reality.

3 years earlier, I had been living with my boyfriend in a remote mining location north of Adelaide. We had come back to Adelaide to celebrate my 21st birthday with a party at my parents' home.

My boyfriend had gone home to get ready whilst I prepared for the party. As he had yet to give me my birthday present, I was silently hoping for an engagement ring.

8pm rolled around and still no sign of my boyfriend. All the guests had arrived but him. 9pm and still no sign of my boyfriend. At 9:30pm, he turned up. He invited me to come outside where he wanted to talk to me in private. I was so excited.

DISCOVERING MY GIFT

"Marion," he said, "I want you to move out of our flat as I have someone else that I want to have move in with me."

Wait. What?

My thoughts were racing. Get to the part about asking me to marry you, would you? Interrupting my thoughts, my now ex-boyfriend asked me if I had heard him. Again he said, "I want you to move out of our flat as I have someone else that I want to have move in with me."

Yeah, alright, I heard you the first time buddy.

The ground fell away from beneath my feet. I was gutted. Absolutely gutted. Happy 21st, Marion. As suddenly as he had arrived, he was gone, leaving me devastated and in shock. I went back into the party, drank half a bottle of Bundaberg Rum (which I still to this day cannot stand the smell of) and went into my bedroom crying my heart out.

How could I not have seen this coming? Had I just chosen to ignore the signs? In hindsight, all the signs had been there. I had chosen to ignore them, to take the risk and stay with him despite knowing he was seeing other women behind my back. Because after all, I didn't want to end up on the shelf. Perhaps that's why I took him back two years later.

After moving back into my parents' house, my Dad asked me what I wanted to do with my life. I told him I wanted to skydive and get paid to travel. I mean, who wouldn't? So I learnt how to skydive. I also applied for and won a job living and working as a waitress on board the beautiful Murray River Explorer and Murray River Queen vessels in South Australia. I followed this up with work as a Hostess / Cook for the Ansett Pioneer bus company. I took Barramundi fishing tours throughout the Northern Territory and Queensland for up to 25 days at a time. Life was good.

It was during one of the breaks between fishing tours that my ex-boyfriend called in to see me at home. No mobile phones or Facebook in those days, things were done face to face.

Answering the doorbell one day, I was greeted with a beautiful bunch of red roses and the face I had loved two years earlier. He was back. Now that I think about it, I don't remember ever receiving an apology from him. But I took him back anyway.

To cut a long story short, we bought a house and moved in. Organised a wedding date, chose the venue and the dress. Invitations were written. Then one day I came home to find his Mum at the kitchen sink knee deep in washing up. All the cupboard doors were open. She was washing everything, which seemed a little odd.

My boyfriend greeted me and asked me to come into our bedroom to talk. Oh God, not again. Alas, again I heard those stinging words that he seemed to say so easily, "Marion, I want you to move out of our house as I have someone else that I want to have move in with me."

Really, the exact same words?

"I want you to move out of our flat as I have someone else that I want to have move in with me."

Jesus, he really loves saying that doesn't he...

In retrospect I wondered why I accepted his decision

without a fight. But I knew deep down why. Because I'd already known we were never going to get married. He was not right for me. How could someone who loved himself more than he loved anyone or anything else love me?

I had ignored the signs again. So, again I had to learn the hard way. Life is after all, a spiritual training ground. This time it was harder though, much harder. I was now 25 years old and had to move back into my parents' home after having had a decent taste of independence. To that point I was never that close to my parents, and to move back home to an environment that I did not feel supported in made me feel incredibly lonely.

In retrospect I know my parents were only doing the best they could. I know they were concerned for me and probably thought the advice they were giving me was the best thing for me. But at the time being told to pretend my boyfriend had died so that I could stop thinking about him was hard to swallow. How do you do that anyway, when you are still in love with that person? You can't just switch love off. I couldn't anyway. It nearly killed me, literally.

My boyfriend had always called me fat. I weighed 53 kilograms. I know, special guy right? He was the type of guy that spent a lot of time flirting with other girls. I took it very personally, who wouldn't? He was never one for giving me compliments, but always complimented other girls in front of me. Why did I ignore the signs?

I spent the next two years in self-loathing as an anorexic/bulimic purging all my anxiety, depression and hatred towards the world and myself many times a day. My weight plummeted to 47kgs. I was on my own here. Alone and lonely.

And so, I found myself on the edge of this cliff. I had never felt so low in my life. I sobbed. I screamed. I yelled aloud, "When will I meet someone who will love me for me?"

Then a voice cut the air and said, "Next Year."

Had it not felt so profound, I would probably have laughed.

"Next Year," the voice said again. It was a very real and audible voice. I looked around to see if anyone had snuck into my car but I was in the middle of nowhere. No one lived there or ever went there. There was nothing there. There was no one in my car.

And suddenly the crying and sobbing was over and I was filled with the most amazing sensation of unconditional love and a feeling that everything really would be ok.

Exactly 12 months later, I met my husband at a skydiving weekend in Canberra. We were married for 25 years.

The Thunderstorm

Ever since that day on the cliff, I'd wanted to know more about that voice. A few years later I got my answers.

Anyone who knew me knew that I was terrified of thunderstorms. Even as an adult, I would cower under the quilt on the bed blocking my ears and jumping out of my skin with every lightning bolt and crack of thunder. That

DISCOVERING MY GIFT

was until one evening during the winter of 1990.

My husband was working an afternoon shift and the big gates at the front of our driveway were shut. The rain was bucketing down and the sky was illuminated with back-to-back flashes of lightning. The thunder sounded and felt like it was six feet above the roof of the house. The house vibrated with every thunderclap.

It was my worst nightmare. I had never experienced a storm like this before. My bed felt very safe and that was right where I planned to stay. Or so I thought.

Suddenly and inexplicably, I felt an overwhelming urge to get out of bed. I still cannot really understand what happened next but it was certainly my Spiritual awakening! I walked through the house in the dark, illuminated only by the lightning cutting through the sky. I was operating completely on remote control. I was being guided by an unseen, loving presence into my lounge room. I was physically forced to sit in the lounge chair by the window where the blinds were open. Oddly, I felt no fear. In fact, I felt calmer than I ever had before.

Outside, the wind was howling. The lightning and thunder were insistent on keeping everyone awake that night. Yet, I was calm. I asked myself what I was doing and reminded myself that I was petrified of thunderstorms. Why on earth was I sitting in the lounge room during the storm of the century without any fear? If anything, I felt an incredible feeling of safety and protection. The whole situation felt very surreal.

Then suddenly, I heard an audible voice. It was mine. I

had begun talking aloud, yet the words were foreign to me. What was going on?

"Marion, I am your Opa. I have your other Opa here too. And Joop, your uncle. We are your Guides. We will walk through your life with you, guiding you at every turn. You need to start working with people on a spiritual level, helping them to find the love within themselves and share it with their family and friends."

Opa went on to say, "You have a very special Gift. The gift of helping people. Helping their Souls. By helping them on a Soul level, you help them on a human level. The world is so out of balance and it is for our own spiritual evolvement that we guide you for your spiritual evolvement. As Souls, we all have jobs to do. Once you pass over, you too, will be a Guide for people remaining alive. However, you are needed to start doing your spiritual job now. This is your training ground."

"What is my job?" I asked.

"You will help put families' lives back in order, one family at a time. You have been given the Gift of psychic awareness and universal wisdom. We will bring people to you who are troubled. We will give you the words they need to hear. You will make a real difference in so many lives. Whilst you may not realise it now, they will."

I continued to speak aloud, "Marion, you know there is more to life than what you can see. Know this; Souls are as real as human bodies. Souls just want to love and be loved. Humans complicate their lives with their egos. Attitude, anger, competitiveness, materialism, gossiping, jealousy and distrust. This has thrown the world off balance. We are your support, your Team here above the clouds. We walk with you and next to you. We will guide you. Please trust us. We know you understand. We know that you feel that what we are saying is true."

"We all come into each other's lives as either a Teacher or a Student. We all come in at different levels in the Spiritual School called Life. Some come in at a level comparable to senior high school or university. Other's come in at a Kindergarten level. Some do this during their incarnation on earth, others, once they've passed over, as a Guide."

"It is the role of the Teacher in the upper levels to live and teach spiritual lessons by being an example to those in the lower levels. These lessons become evident when you stop and realise why you are constantly clashing with someone on a human level. At all times ask yourself, 'which Spiritual value am I meant to be demonstrating or teaching here? Is it forgiveness; tolerance; patience; charity; unconditional love; compassion or trust?'. Whilst you are a Teacher, you too will learn from others. You will also teach others how to teach others and how to learn from others. Our Souls know that they are here to evolve. To get closer to the omniscient source of unconditional love. To rid ourselves of our egos and return to love, return to the Soul."

"Let us Guide you, we need you to do our work for us on earth. We will guide you and provide you with all the tools and spiritual knowledge you need in order to do the work of your Soul. Your life will never be the same after tonight".

CAUGHT BETWEEN TWO WORLDS

I started to come back into the room, reluctantly leaving the feeling of intense peace and love that I had just experienced. Everything felt so surreal. I felt so calm. Suddenly, I knew what I needed to do in my life.

I realised that the storm outside had intensified. I was no longer frightened. Surprising myself, I walked outside into the storm to open the gates for my husband who would soon be coming home from afternoon shift. Just as I was opening the gates, standing in the pelting rain, my husband drove in the driveway. When he got out after parking the car, he looked at me, astonished by finding me outside opening the gates for him.

"Why are you outside in the storm, you hate storms!"

"I wanted to open the gates for you so that you could drive straight in".

"Yes, but why? You hate storms and here you are outside in one. Are you ok?"

"Yes I am more than ok". I tried to explain what I had just experienced but was unable to find the words.

I am no longer scared of storms. In fact, I look forward to them, always hoping for another visit from my Team. Face your fears and you will benefit in ways you could never imagine existed. Fear keeps us away from knowing and honouring our true selves.

I could have cowered under the quilt that night but I did not. I trusted that I would be ok.

I used to wonder whether I missed my calling as a nun but after having my first boyfriend, I knew the convent was no place for me. I know now that we are all Spirits having a human experience and humans having a Spiritual experience. Some of us live in our Souls 50-70% of the time and the others live in their Souls as low as 2-5% of the time. This explains quite simply why we clash. There is more to us than flesh and blood.

As I reflect on that night, 36 years ago, I can confirm that my Team were right about one thing and that was that my life would never be the same after that night. It never was. That night had added a completely new dimension to my life. For the better.

Mark

Over the years that followed, I often found myself talking aloud to my Team whenever I needed guidance. I would talk or pray to them daily. I involved them in all aspects of my life. I would talk to them about my problems out loud. They would then talk through me, providing me with advice and direction.

Talking aloud is in fact one of the first signs of spiritual development because it is often the case that Spirits talk back through you, providing you with solutions to problems you are enduring. I began walking and talking all the time, often for hours on end, just so I could ask all my questions. I had a few favourite parks that I used to explore. This was the best way for me to hear my Team, free from distractions and interferences.

One day I asked my Team exactly who my Guides were. I was told that there was Opa (my Dad's Father) and

Opa (my Mum's Father). There was also Joop (my Mum's brother) and Mark. Mark was a new Guide. He told me that it was for his own soul's evolvement that he had attached to guide me through my life. Mark explained to me that it was in my Soul's best interest to listen to him. He reiterated that a time would come when I too would pass over and become a Guide to another's life. Mark was once in human form, just like my other Guides.

Over the years, Mark and my Team have guided me through many a sticky personal situation and many Readings. Without them, I would not have experienced and learnt all that I have. I would never have written this book. I intend to thank them personally for sticking by me through all the tough times, even when I was ignoring them - thinking I knew better. I am only just starting to learn that there is no shortcut through life's tough lessons and that I'll keep learning until all my fingers are the same length! I came up with that saying years ago. It makes a lot of sense if you think about it.

Staven (Understanding Ouija Boards)

My parents have communicated with their own Guides using a Ouija board for many years. Their motivation to do so was for their own spiritual growth and development. The first time I sat with them, I was introduced to the latest member of my Team, Staven.

Staven told me he was my Healer. He encouraged me to use my hands for healing my family and friends, explaining that he would provide healing from above through them.

Later, I was encouraged to do Reiki courses and offer healing to those drawn to it. Reiki is one of those wonderful therapies that will work whether you believe in it or not. It offers great comfort to the terminally ill as well as to those who's Souls are tired. Universal love and healing is transferred via the laying on of hands to the recipient. Whilst it may not provide physical healing, it certainly offers comfort. Many patients say that sleep and peace of mind are improved after a session of Reiki.

Many contemplate using a Ouija board out of curiosity. They can be a very useful educational tool; however, be sure to use it with someone who has used it before and understands the laws around protection and interpretation of messages. For one thing, it is essential that you engage a Gatekeeper as protection. Gatekeepers literally allow in the good and keep out the bad. This is very important. Before you begin using the Ouija board, ensure that you say a prayer of protection for all those present. Ouija boards are not games and should never be used without supervision or training.

Before you delve in tools like Ouija boards, my advice is to consider the power of prayer. For centuries people have prayed aloud. Whether at home or in church, they hope those above the clouds hear them. In time, prayers are answered, depending on what we have prayed for, of course. Praying with good intention and motivation will bring you closer to spiritual enlightenment and peace. Praying from your Ego requesting monetary or materialistic benefits won't work. You have to work for these!

You do not need Ouija boards or tarot cards to hear or understand messages from your Spirit Guides. If you feel these tools will benefit you to help you interpret messages, use them. It may be a good way for you to learn to trust what you are hearing. Then over time, you may find that you no longer use them and can adjust your own internal radio settings to hear messages loud and clear.

I recommend finding time every day or every second day that is just for you! Go for a walk in nature and talk to your Guides. We all have them. One day you too will be a Guide to someone on earth, so engage with your Spirit Guide. They are as real as you and I. If you prefer to, put on some nice music and just relax. You do not have to call it prayer. Call it talking to your best friend. Invite them into the room to be with you. You will feel a little weird at first talking to the empty chair in the room and wonder if it is your imagination playing tricks on you when you start receiving guidance. Just trust. Ask for proof that only you know.

Remember, too, that we don't always like what we hear but we are always given what we need. Additionally, if you are going to ask for messages, be sure to quieten yourself in order to hear them. Look for the signposts all around you in your life. They will direct you to your request.

If a Spirit was to manifest itself in front of you at your request for proof, you would most likely drop dead out of sheer fright. Thus, spirits cannot do this for obvious reasons. What they can do is come to us in our dreams or automatic writing to guide us. They can show us signs, send us smells, play songs on the radio, and bring people to us that can help us with our prayers. This is how Spirit Guides make contact with and guide us.

Just Knowing – Trusting Your Instinct

Every Mum thinks their baby is the cutest. I was no different. So, when I saw an advertisement in the paper for an upcoming "Cutest Baby of the Year Competition" in June 1992, my sixth sense told me that my son would win and that I should enter him into it.

I told my husband about the competition and that I would enter our son into it and that we would come home with the trophy. I received no response. I told my Mum about the competition and that I would enter our son into it and that we would come home with the trophy. Mum said she would love to come along.

Three months later, my husband and father were out working by the pool. Mum and I went and said goodbye. "Where are you going?" they asked. "To pick up our son's trophy for winning the Cutest Baby of the Year. I received no response.

I cannot explain it but I just knew our son would win. When we arrived at the shopping centre, there were so many well-behaved cute babies. And our son just cried and grizzled the whole time. However, I still knew we would be going home with the trophy that day. Sure enough, we did.

***

The kids were aged one and two. Interest rates were 17%. We were a single income family and it was time for me to go back to work. But I had no suitable clothes and no money to pay for them. I asked the universe to help me start the ball rolling to go back to work.

So, when I saw a promotion for a competition at the local shopping centre, again, I just knew I would win. The timing was perfect. Apparently, all someone had to do was stand in the right spot at the local mall between 2pm and 3pm and you would win $50. I knew exactly where that spot was!

I needed a new skirt and blouse to start working again, so I packed the kids up and headed to the mall. An hour later, I walked out with the $50 and headed to Kmart to buy myself the skirt and blouse I needed to go back to work. I'd put out to the universe that I needed these things and the universe answered my call. If your request to the universe is genuine, it will answer your call.

Bill In Sydney

My ex-husband and I were travelling to Sydney to meet with a man we were considering going into business with. His name was Bill and we'd never met him before, nor seen a photo of him.

The flight was non eventful but rather than race to disembark the plane once we had docked at the terminal, I

DISCOVERING MY GIFT

reached for the sick bag in the seat pocket in front of me. I was overcome with fear and felt the urge to vomit.

My ex-husband asked me what was wrong. I told him that as we were landing I had a vision of us in Bill's car stopped right in the middle of a busy intersection in Parramatta. Bill had driven through red traffic lights and once I'd pointed it out to him, he stopped smack bang right in the centre. The vision felt extremely real. In his usual style, my ex-husband fobbed off my vision as nonsense.

We claimed our baggage and moved outside to wait for Bill to pick us up. My ex said, "I don't know what kind of car Bill has or what he looks like!" I immediately said, "It's a Toyota Land Cruiser and it's white." Then, I proceeded to describe Bill to him also. I described Bill as looking like an absent minded professor, highly intelligent, scatterbrained and dishevelled. I proceeded to continue to describe to him what their house looked like. My ex then rang Bill to find out what kind of car we should be looking out for and repeated aloud what Bill was saying on the phone, "A Toyota Land Cruiser – and it's white."

A few minutes later, Bill drove up in his white Land Cruiser and we hopped in. He was a really likeable chap. His driving, however, was atrocious. He was really living up to the image I had of him of an absent minded professor.

I was sitting in the back passenger seat, perched between the two front seats.

"Bill, STOP!" I screamed. Bill hit the brakes and brought the car to a stop right in the middle of the inter-

CAUGHT BETWEEN TWO WORLDS

section. He had just driven through red lights! I said "The lights are red!"

I punched my Ex in the arm. "See," I said, "SEE!" Of course, he didn't respond.

I found myself reaching for a non-existent sick bag while Bill laughed off the near miss. When you receive warnings as a premonition, please make sure you listen to them. They could just save your life. There was absolutely nothing I could do about that vision, it was out of my control. But it did come true.

The Break-In

When our children were young, money was very tight. Any spare money we had, I hid in a tin. This tin was kept in a cupboard. We relied on this money for treats and special occasions. One day, my Team told me to take the money out of the box and put it in our bedside cupboard. When I went to hide the money in my bedside cupboard they said, "No, the other one, on your husband's side." I obeyed without thinking, just trusting.

About one month later, I was asked to work late. My boss came to me and asked me to complete a report which meant that I would have to work an additional two hours.

Normally, I would finish work at 3 PM and pick up the children from school. I rang my husband and asked him to collect the children. Once my work was done at 5:30pm, I headed home. When I turned up my street, I saw a police car outside of our house. Fear set in.

DISCOVERING MY GIFT

I drove up to the house and parked my car. My husband walked out of the house towards me and said, "Marion, I'm so sorry. The house has been broken into. All our savings are gone. The box with the money in it was ransacked," He looked distraught. He knew how hard things had been for us financially after moving from Adelaide to Perth with two very young children.

By this time, police had followed my husband out of the house. Suddenly, I started laughing most inappropriately. My husband looked confused. I said to him, "It's okay, it's okay," and took his hand, leading him back into the house.

"What do you mean it's okay?"

"Come with me," I said, as I led him to the bedroom. I was smiling big, thinking about my Team's recent instructions regarding the money.

As I went into our bedroom, I looked at my bedside cupboard and saw that the door was open. Of course it was. However, when I went over to my husband's bedside cupboard, the door was still closed. Of course it was.

"What are you doing?" asked my husband.

"Look," I said as I opened his bedside cupboard door and took out the money that I had hidden there some weeks before

"Why is it in there?" he asked in shock.

"You wouldn't believe it even if I told you. A couple of weeks ago my Team told me to move the money from the box. When I went to put it inside my bedside cupboard, Opa instructed yours instead. Now we know why."

My husband didn't know what to say. The policeman

came in and asked what was going on. I simply told him that I had hid some money in the cupboard and was checking to see if it was still there.

We then went into the kitchen to survey the remaining contents of the tin strewn across the kitchen floor. If the money had still been where we'd had it, it would have been stolen. That money was really important to us at the time. Had I not listened to my Opa, our savings would have been stolen that day. That box had been in the same cupboard for two years until that point. It was a really good hiding spot. But I am glad that I trusted Opa's message that day. I was learning more and more to trust those kinds of messages.

Helene's House In England

We all have people in our lives that we have an immediate connection with. Helene was one of those people for me. She is 20 years older than me and when I looked at her, I saw my future self. She always said that likewise, when she looked at me, she saw her past self.

Helene was a Homeopath and also worked with Bach Flower Remedies. I had never heard of them until I met her. More importantly, she was a spiritual teacher for me. She understood me like few others have. When I was around Helene, I felt normal. She didn't judge me and I could talk to her about anything and everything I experienced. She helped me make sense of it all.

In fact, I think she was the first person to tell me that

what I could do was a gift and that I should use it. Helene gave me the confidence to be me and I will be forever grateful for her grace and wisdom.

At first I visited her as I needed help that I felt western medicine could not provide. Helene gave me some remedies to take for my constitution and nerves. They helped immediately, and still do today. She also gave me remedies for the kids. I was amazed at how quickly they worked and relied on them for years. Because of her, I studied homoeopathy and Bach Flower remedies so that I could further understand their magic.

During one of our sessions, I told Helene about a vision I'd had of an old stonewash white house in a country setting somewhere overseas. I told her it had a hedge all around it and an old wooden fence, slightly ajar. It felt like England to me. It felt special. It was a very vivid vision. Helene said she had no idea what the vision represented or where it might be as she'd never seen it before.

You know what it's like. Life goes on. Kids go to school, we go to work, weeks go by, months go by and suddenly years had gone by before I realised I hadn't heard from Helene for quite a while.

I rang her phone numbers, they'd been disconnected. I went to her home, new tenants had moved in. I looked in the telephone directory, she was no longer listed. My friend had disappeared.

In one way, I was envious of her. One thing we had in common was our dislike of living in Perth. It didn't feel like home for either of us. I thought perhaps she'd finally taken the opportunity to move away.

Life went on. Busy, busy, busy. Then, one day I got a surprise in the form of a postcard in my letterbox. Helene was in England, of course. In fact, it wasn't a postcard, it was a photo she had taken of the house her father had lived in in England. It was exactly like the vision I had shared with her years earlier. I felt such joy for her.

We never saw or spoke to each other again. I missed her though, and always carried her in my heart. After my ex-husband asked me for a divorce, I made plans to move back to Adelaide to live. Desperate to talk to her before I moved, I trawled the internet, Facebook and the White Pages for any sign of Helene, hoping that she'd come back to Perth to live. But alas, there was no sign of her. I was saddened to think that I may never see my dear friend again.

Plans were finalised and I was all set for the four day drive across the Nullarbor to start my new life in Adelaide. I popped down to my local shopping mall to pick up some last minute necessities like chocolate, potato chips and soft drink for the journey.

As I entered the double glass doors that led into the mall, I saw a familiar figure looking around at nothing particular. It appeared to me as if she was waiting for someone. It couldn't be, could it? What were the chances? But yes, it was her. It was Helene.

I stood in front of her, looked her in the eye and said to her, "Are you looking for me by any chance?"

"Oh Marion, it's You!"

DISCOVERING MY GIFT

"Helene! It's You! I've been asking the universe to find you for me. I've missed you, where have you been?" I asked

"Oh Marion! It's you! It's really you! Oh how I've missed you. I've got so much to tell you." We hugged and cried, oblivious to those walking past us. In that moment, we were all that mattered.

We walked arm in arm, like good friends do, to find a quiet little table at one of the cafés in the mall. The next hour was spent catching up on all our news, amazed that the universe had orchestrated this meeting for us. And at a shopping centre that Helene never went to, no less.

We felt blessed, an incredible sense of oneness with the universe. We knew then that we would carry each other in our hearts forever no matter where we were in the world.

Dearest Helene, wherever you are when you read this, know that I am forever grateful to have met you. You are my other half. You are my Soul Mate. We are connected by Spirit and our work is Special.

Caught Between Two Worlds: Making Sense of My Gift

Being Caught Between Two Worlds

I think nonstop. I analyse nonstop. It's exhausting. I have been on a crusade my whole life to justify the air I breathe and the space I take up on this earth. I feel Caught between the following sets of Two Worlds:

- Spirituality and Reality
- Depression and Happiness
- Confident and Not confident
- Bi-Polar High and Bi-Polar Low
- Rational and Irrational
- Love and Hate

When I am awake, I am in both worlds. I talk to my Team, asking for their advice out loud and receiving their

MAKING SENSE OF MY GIFT

advice which I also speak out loud. It always makes sense. It's not always in my favour though. Sometimes, I get a telling off. But that's when I switch off (or try to). Of course, that's all in vain because the Team simply try even harder to get through to me.

I look at other people and they seem so normal. I often long to be like them. Sometimes someone will ask me a question about someone else and I will give them answer without blinking or thinking. That's what receiving psychic information is like. It comes through you, it doesn't belong to you.

How could I even know? I wonder this all the time. Why do I need to know about things before they happen or why am I able to finish people's sentences for them when they are lost for words? So often, I have noticed that if someone in my life has come to me to ask me to borrow something, I usually have it in my hand ready to give to them before they've even asked for it.

I find it so very hard to put into words what my life is like. I feel different to everyone else. I don't know what other people feel like but when I'm out and about, I don't hear people talking the way I do. I've always felt like a misfit, in a bad way.

Some Psychics like to glorify the gift. I have a deeper understanding. I have always seemed to get exactly what I needed when I least expected it, not what I wanted when I did expect it. I am blessed. Very blessed, and I know it.

It's also weird. My life is weird. Others relate to my psychic ability as weird, and that's ok. I've learnt to love being weird. I really do. I don't know any different.

Whilst I feel caught between two worlds, I have certainly learnt to balance it and have trained my Gatekeeper above the clouds to keep out the riff raff for me. I struggle to understand and rationalise my human mind. Yet, my Soul understands. And after all, that's what guides me through life.

I feel like I lead a double existence, a parallel universe of sorts. I live in a heightened state of vigilance and awareness all the time. When I'm with someone I watch their every unconscious move. They looked away when I asked them a question that required an honest answer. They touched their ear, that's significant. They cleared their throat at a certain point in our conversation and I've picked up on the subtle meaning of that. They closed their eyes when I asked them an important question. That negated the words they then said.

You see, it's not what people say that I read, it's what they don't say. In the past, mostly in work places, I have experienced face to face jealousy and bullying because of my 'differentness'. Not because of what I do, I tell very few people about that. Just because I'm not like them. I don't fit into their mould of what's normal, and I'm not prepared to stand around gossiping like they do. Therefore, I don't fit in. People can be cruel, and I've experienced situations where people invite me to work functions where they end up belittling me or making fun of me. I've learnt that out of ten people, two or three people will genuinely care about what you say and the other seven will use it against you. They do this so that they can feel better about their own shortcomings.

I interpret every signal people put out (consciously or subconsciously) and take them all personally. I'm always on guard. I guess what I'd like to say to people most of the time is, "Don't judge me. Rather, get to know me. I am really quite likeable. I will listen to your words. But if your body doesn't back up the words you are using, when you say you like me then I will simply withdraw myself from you and save myself for those that really count." There's a difference between being alone and being lonely. I'd rather be on my own than feeling lonely with others.

I share this with you in the hope that you may understand that whilst you might think being psychic is a gift and wish you could do it, it's also a massive burden.

Being Psychic Isn't All Tea and Scones

Our minds are complicated. Our Souls are simple. We just want to love and be loved. It's when these two worlds collide that I get caught between two worlds.

Many years ago when my husband first asked me for a divorce, I begged my Guides to take away my Gift until my kids were older, my husband believed or the house was paid off. I told them that that would be when I would feel ready to do their work for them.

It was hard enough just being me, feeling like I didn't fit in anywhere. I went to endless counselling sessions with Psychologists and Counsellors, but still never felt understood. I was just labelled according to Psychological principles, medicated and left to work out where I fitted in myself.

I've always felt like an outsider looking into other people's worlds but not being allowed to stay as I never felt good enough. I've always envied the lives I saw other people living with their families and friends. Mind you, I've also seen things in other people's lives that I definitely would not want for myself.

Because I know about my unique Psychic abilities, I feel like I over compensate to be seen as normal. To be honest, I've felt over the years that it would be easier to be gay and come out to family and friends. I mean absolutely no disrespect to the gay community with that comment. I have many gay friends, all of them very comfortable with themselves and their lives. I'm simply trying to make a comparison about how difficult it has been to be this way. In many ways I identify with the gay community because I sure know what it's like to be unfairly labelled as an outcast.

Tell the wrong person you are a Psychic and/or Medium and suddenly the whole energy in that conversation has changed and you feel judged, even threatened. Certainly not accepted. I want to trust the people I meet and what they're saying but my psychic radar gives me other signals.

I used to think I was extremely paranoid. Now, I realise that it's an ability to see straight through people's lies. Being this way has made me an extremely shy, self-conscious and insecure person. Surprised? You needn't be. I've perfected a face that I show the world, but I feel much safer and happier when I'm in my own environment where I don't have to worry about what people think of me.

I find communicating hard. I've always adapted myself to each person I am talking to in order to be the person I think they want me to be because I could pick up things they didn't like about me. So, during the conversation, I would try and change those nuances. I've always felt I had to hide the psychic side of me because as mentioned before, it's not acceptable dinner table conversation.

Some days I think I'd like to stay home for the rest of my life. I mentioned feeling paranoid earlier. Feeling paranoid is the absolute worst. It feels so real and makes you want to run away and hide. You feel like everyone has a secret they know about you but won't let you in on it. My perceived paranoia is one of the main motivations behind the title of this book. I guess it's what I've been trying to describe all along.

Even when I do receive the reassurance I need, I still question the validity of it. Are you just telling me what I want to hear or do you mean what you are saying? It's never enough. I know self-worth needs to come from within and that's obviously my Spiritual lesson in life. And in saying that, when I'm wearing my Soul hat, I have no problems.

Mind vs Soul

People have said to me in the past "How can you possibly provide Spiritual guidance or counselling when you yourself have your own mental health issues?" Having my own mental health issues has in fact given me significant insight into what other people go through. In asking that, they are referring to my mind. There's a lot more to us than just our minds. I've been called emotional. I'm not, I'm passionate. I've been told I'm too sensitive. Well, what do you expect? I am a Psychic after all. That's how we do our work. We sense.

People often comment that it must be draining listening to people's problems all day, trying to help them. It would be, but I don't do that. I work on a very deep soul level. I don't touch the mind, it's way too complicated. I'll leave that to the professionals. And in that way, when I read someone, I become energised, not drained.

Universal information comes through with unconditional love. It's actually an amazing feeling. Once you've touched it, you never forget it. Working on a soul level is actually quite simple. Working with beautiful spiritual values like: Love, Forgiveness, Tolerance, Compassion, Empathy, Generosity, Grace, Peace and Serenity is beautiful. Work with an Omniscient Life Source cannot be compared to working with the mind.

When you live Spiritually, Soulfully and Mindfully - aware of your Karma and spiritual responsibilities - you do not end up with a lot of baggage to carry around through your life. You have lived in the moment, made the best decision you could at the time, with the information available to you. And then moved on. When you live

MAKING SENSE OF MY GIFT

Mindfully and Spiritually, there is no residue.

Baggage Handlers (my term for mental health professionals) get to work with the mind and its emotions, thoughts and behaviour patterns. Upbringing, belief systems and ego's are all addressed by Baggage Handlers. In that respect, seeing as I have my own pieces of baggage to carry around, I do not see myself as qualified to be your Baggage Handler.

Therefore, when you come to see me for a reading, I invite your ego (mind) to stay outside with mine and compare notes or go for a walk. That way our Souls can enjoy a cuppa and work at a relaxed, uncomplicated Spiritual level.

Why I Read – The Psychic Postie

I look forward to every Reading as a learning opportunity. I look forward to bringing through messages from your guides and loved ones, whether passed or living. There's really no difference, as we are all energy here to encourage our spiritual growth and awareness.

People sometimes ask how it actually works. That will mostly become clear through the Reading examples you'll read in part two of this book. But to reiterate what I've already mentioned, the information doesn't come from me. It comes through me from my Team.

My Team consists of my Dad's Dad (Opa B – He acts as Gatekeeper), my Mum's Dad (Opa D), my Mum's brother (Joop) and my own Guide (Mark) and Healer

(Staven). My Team provide me with the information, I'm just your Psychic Postie. I deliver the mail to you from the mail room above the clouds.

When the mail comes through, it first needs to be sorted. Opa B is my Gatekeeper and he ensures that he gets all names from those wishing to come through with messages for you. This way we can keep control over who comes through and who gets turned away.

Before you come to me for a Reading, I let Opa B and the Team know. They put up a flashing neon sign that says "now accepting mail for 'Adam'. Suddenly every one that has ever known an Adam (not necessarily you) will give their name to Opa B before they are allowed to have a look through the window to see if you are their Adam. This is why at the beginning of the Reading some names may not mean anything to you. However, as the Reading goes on, people connected to you will come through.

During the Reading, my Opa will show me a flash card with a name of a person either alive or passed that would like to make contact with you. Contact is usually very brief. It can be a smile, or anyone of 'I'm sorry', 'I love you', 'I'm proud of you' or 'you are stronger than you realise'. It's not a conversation like you had whilst they were alive. It's a reconnection. It's a way of building your faith to help get you through this life that you know, first hand, that there really is more to life than what you can see, smell, hear and touch.

As the Psychic Postie, I deliver all sorts of mail. It may be a love letter or a perfumed letter from Grandma. It may be junk mail or even hate mail. It might be marked Private and Confidential, in which case, I am not allowed to open it. It's for your discovery at a later date. Other mail may come through wrapped as a surprise package that you can unwrap also at a later date.

That's why I do this work. Because without Psychic Mediums like me, you wouldn't receive these messages.

PART TWO:
Readings

What a Psychic Reading Can and Can't Tell You

Before I recount the most profound Readings I've ever been a part of, I feel it's necessary to outline some basics of the Reading process.

Have you ever gone into a Psychic Reading with high expectations only to be disappointed afterwards? You may have had a burning question that needed a yes or no answer. On the other hand, maybe there was a tough decision or situation in your life that you had to come to terms with. Regardless of the situation, Psychic Readings can provide insight, but it's important to remember that they cannot do the hard work or learn the lessons for you.

When you go to the supermarket to buy one particular item, chances are you will walk out with the item and a whole lot of other items you don't need and maybe even without the initial item itself. However, if you take a list, the chances of coming out with exactly what you needed are greatly increased. I tell people that coming for a Psychic Reading is the same. Bring your list of questions and/

WHAT A READING CAN AND CAN'T TELL YOU

or photos for me to Read. Otherwise, I'll wander the aisles of your mind giving you detergent and sponges, but no chocolate!

If you have never had a Reading before and feel scared about having one, don't be. Were you to come and see me, I would put you at ease right from the start. I love just chatting about you and your spiritual journey. Together we would piece together the messages that come through for you and fit them into the puzzle that is your life

A Psychic Reading can tell you a lot. It can reveal the energy around a particular situation, including the possibilities of what may occur. If you are looking to know when or how you may meet your partner for example, a Psychic can give you suggestions as to the circumstances around when or where you are more likely to find love and romance. Readings can also help you interpret impressions and signs that you yourself receive. Had any strange or confusing dreams lately? A Reading can help you understand their message. Maybe you need clarity on how you feel about something you have been going through but don't understand it? A Psychic Reading can bring clarity and direction. Maybe you aren't sure how a special person feels about you? A Reading can examine the emotional energy around the situation and give you clues.

Finally, a Psychic Reading can tell you about yourself. It can confirm those personality traits that you already know about, while introducing you to sides of yourself that you may not be aware of. It can highlight your strengths and point out your weaknesses. A Reading may provide a shortcut towards a direction you have been working towards, saving you precious time and energy. Hopefully, too, a Reading will provide you with faith and insight into the reasons why you are leading the life you are. Or, perhaps, why you might need to reconsider it.

Yet, a Psychic Reading cannot tell you everything. Which is probably a good thing. Come on, would you really want to know it all? Life is about choices and surprises. Having all the info is like cheating on a test, in the end you only cheat yourself. Seeking spiritual guidance for yourself affords you the opportunity to gain clarification, direction, information and confirmation. It does not give you all the answers. In that way, A Psychic Reading cannot tell you when you are going to die, as handy as that would be.

Another popular question concerns winning money. Of course, we would all love to know about that one! What you need to ask yourself is, if a Psychic could tell you that from a Reading, wouldn't they do it for themselves? They can let you know if they see money coming or finances improving but to a degree, we all make our own luck. Remember though, winning money can create a whole other set of problems.

What about love, I hear you say. A Psychic Reading cannot promise to bring that special someone to you or make anyone fall in love with you. As lovely as that would be, each of us has the free will to choose a partner. A Reading can sense someone's feelings for you or give you advice about approaching a person, but the true magic is up to those people involved. I can tell you if you are going to

WHAT A READING CAN AND CAN'T TELL YOU

meet someone and maybe even how or when and what they look like, but isn't that a bit like finding out the sex of your baby before it's born? We don't get many true surprises in our life. Why not let love find you?

Lastly, a Psychic Reading cannot make decisions for you or tell you what to do. If you have a tough choice to make in life, it's up to you. You can't tell me what to have for lunch, but you can recommend a great snack bar. Spiritual Guidance is the same. I cannot tell you what to do, but I can recommend what to do.

People's lives fall apart soon after they lose sight of the fact that they are in control of it. A Reading can give you information to help you make an informed decision, but when it comes right down to it, you are ultimately responsible. Again, it is a matter of karma and respect. A Reading can help you understand the choices and consequences, but cannot walk the path for you. There are many roads to the same destination.

Your life is your journey. It must be done one-step at a time. Just like a book - one chapter at a time. If it is direction you are looking for, then I can look ahead through your book and direct you so that you do not waste precious years focusing on the wrong career choice. Psychic Readings can provide you a wealth of information and help you along life's journey. Although they cannot tell you which road to take, they can help you navigate it better.

James: A Child In Turmoil

Dedicated to my son, James.

As a parent of a five year old, I thought James' behaviour was normal. I just thought James was still going through the terrible twos at five! It wasn't until I started getting phone calls from the school asking me to meet with them to discuss his behaviour that I realised all the temper tantrums and destructive behaviour we had been seeing at home were not normal and were being replicated at school.

No wonder James was never invited to friends' houses to play. The kids from school were scared of him and the parents worried that he would influence their child. I even had another mum say exactly that to my face when I asked if her son would like to come over after school one day.

I really felt for my son. No one wanted to be his friend, which of course made me sad. I kept hoping that someone would invite him back to his or her house to play. However, no one ever did. It is still very difficult for me to talk about the tantrums and screaming, because I have never ever seen another child act out so violently. It was scary to watch. I felt like I was losing my son and part of me felt it was my fault. I was still new in Perth and trying to make friends who had kids that could play with mine. However, with this type of behaviour, no one wanted to know us.

My son was a very loving child, and I loved him dearly, but I did not like his behaviour. At one point I even told my husband that I couldn't do it anymore and was thinking about walking out on the whole family. I never did and am now glad that I didn't. It really would have made everything much worse.

None of what the teachers were telling me was a surprise to me. I still have all the daily and weekly reports that were sent home at the time. I had also been seeing all the evidence at home. Temper tantrums, yelling, throwing things, hitting his sister and us with a strength that seemed to be greater than he should have at that age. Needless to say, I was worried.

His preschool teacher was constantly calling us in to have meetings with the counsellor, principal and herself. At these meetings, we were confronted with facts about what our son's behaviour was like in the classroom towards his classmates and teachers. It was suggested at these meetings that we get our son tested for Attention Deficit Hyperactivity Disorder (ADHD). It was also suggested that if we did not follow this path of intervention, he would be expelled from school. He was five years old for goodness sake! How many five year olds do you know that are expelled from school? Apparently our son. It was intolerable for all of us because of the intensity and relentlessness.

As his Mum, I had a sense that there was more to his behaviour. I took him to Paediatricians, Psychologists, ADD and ADHD Specialists, Allergy Specialists, Nutritionists, Counsellors and numerous doctors. Following months of intense testing, it was deemed that my son did not have anything wrong with him. Nothing that could be diagnosed anyway. Whilst, I was prepared to take him to all this mainstream testing, I instinctively knew that there was something more sinister at play. I still wanted to be seen as doing all the right things, attending all the normal places my husband and school suggested I take him to for help. But I knew it wasn't going to work. I needed someone else I could talk to about his struggles.

How could I even begin to ask for help other than what he'd been receiving? I didn't know where to turn. Back then, I had never seen anyone else go through what I was. But boy, I sure have since.

Eighteen months prior, I had been invited to a spiritualist circle group evening. I went with a friend I had just met, but knew no one else there. As soon as I walked in the door, my Opa said to me "Marion, see that lady over there in the corner with the brown coat and brown hair? You need to get her name and phone number by the end of the night."

"Why?" I asked.

"One day you will know. Keep her details in a very safe

place".

To myself, I thought, "How am I going to get her name and phone number? I've never even spoken to this woman before."

The evening itself was quite boring. I now understand that the only reason I went there was to get this woman's details. At the time I still wasn't sure why I needed them, but I trusted my Opa enough to ensure that I left that night with Jaqueline's contact details.

Soon enough, it became clearer why I needed them. One Wednesday afternoon in June 1997, I was at home taking care of our daughter when the phone rang.

"Marion, this is the principal of James's school. I require you to come to school to pick up your son. He has been expelled."

When I asked why, the principal replied "you will see when you come to my office," and he promptly hung up. Clearly something was very wrong. For some time I had feared that my son had three bad entities/energies, also known as spirits, attached to him. What I didn't know was what to do next.

I arrived at the school and headed straight for the principal's office, avoiding making eye contact with the office staff, who shied away from greeting me. I was shaking and felt like a naughty child myself when I knocked on the door. The principal beckoned me into his office, which I could clearly see now had been properly trashed. The principal was a very big man. He would have been six foot tall and almost six foot wide as well! He said to me "Marion, what is going on with your son? This is what James's done to my office. In the process, he even knocked me to the ground, and I'm a big guy! We've chosen to expel James. He would not be allowed back until we saw significant change in his behaviour. Please get help for him and your family."

While I was speaking to the principal, my son had been cowering under the heavy mahogany desk, which was the only thing left standing in the room. I motioned to him that it was safe for him to come to me and he did. He looked so small and scared.

I took his little hand in mine, left the Principal's office and the school behind, and headed to the sanctuary of our home. When my husband got home that afternoon, I recounted the story for him. He couldn't believe it. Had things really gotten this bad? There was no denying that anymore.

We were both so upset. I had already tried everything I could to get a diagnosis for James in order to get him help and/or medication. All to no avail. Everyone I had taken him to had given the same answer: "we cannot find anything wrong with your son, he is a normal 5 year old."

That clearly wasn't true, which I knew but had ignored for too long. It was then that I chose to act on my knowledge of the bad entities attached to him. It was the only cause of his behaviour that we hadn't properly investigated. How did I know they were they were there? I just did. But, that didn't mean I knew how to deal with them or how to fix him. In fact, I didn't understand any of it. Psychically I just knew they were wrecking my son's life and our lives along with it.

Of course, my human mind questioned if this could even be possible. Sure, I had seen movies where bad entities took over bodies, but that was the movies. This was real life. This was my son's life. This was our life.

I had never heard of or known about any other child suffering this way. I tried to talk to my husband about my fears but it soon became clear that I was on my own. I understood his point of view, but I was scared. I can't even begin to describe the desperation I felt as a Mum at this point.

I rang my Mum in Adelaide and told her about the events leading up to the expulsion. I could hear the anguish in her voice. Mum also knew that my fears were real. Very real and very possible.

I couldn't talk to the Mum's at school. I couldn't talk to my husband. I couldn't talk to the school counsellor, even though it was a Catholic school. So I confided in my best friend Nairina.

I met Nairina at playgroup. I knew the day I met her that we were destined to be good friends. We were actually never good friends, we were great friends. Nairina had seen my son's behaviour first hand on many occasions and had admitted to me that it certainly seem uncontrollable and out of line for a normal five year old. She had also seen me leave playgroup on a few occasions because of his destructive tantrums and screaming, after spoiling the fun for others. On these occasions, all I could do was apologise to all profusely, bundle him and his sister up, carry him out to the car, and go home.

Whilst Nairina could not understand what I was going through, she never judged me and stood by me every step of the way. Without her, I do not know how I would have coped. She gave me the support my husband could not.

So James and I were heading into unchartered waters. I took time off work to stay home with my son. One day, as clear as day, I knew that I had to find the piece of paper on which I had written down the name and phone number of a woman that I had collected eighteen months earlier. Just like Opa had asked me to, I had kept it in a safe place. Not knowing why, but trusting the message nonetheless.

With a feeling of complete calmness and trust, I dialled the number. A woman answered.

"Hello, may I speak with Jacqueline please?" I said.

"This is Jacqueline. How did you know about my son?" she replied.

"I don't know about your son, I only know about my son," I said.

"Tell me what's going on" said Jacqueline.

Instinctively, I did not want to tell Jacqueline about my fears regarding the entities. I wanted to see what she would find out herself. I knew I could trust her, but at first only told her that my son had been expelled from school that day. I then asked her to be patient with me and I told her the story about how I came about her phone number and how I knew I could trust the message about ringing her.

Jacqueline listened patiently, then asked me for my

phone number and told me she would be in touch over the next few days.

The following evening, Jacqueline rang back. She sounded exhausted.

"Hi Marion, it's Jacq," she said.

"Hi Jacq, how are you? You sound exhausted," I replied.

"How's James doing?" she asked. "Have you noticed any change?"

I told her that James had spent the afternoon watching TV quietly by himself whilst his sister was at school. What she said next threw me momentarily.

"There were two entities attached to James, but I've worked with them and they've agreed to leave him alone."

"What does that mean?" I asked.

"Well, there's a certain kind of person in this world. You know, the kind that would beat a bus driver while he's stopped and then steal his money, usually while high on drugs."

And then Jacqueline took a deep sigh and paused. I couldn't wait to hear where this was all going.

"…well when they die, they don't automatically go to the place we might call heaven like you do at the end of what would have been the term of your natural life. They stay in a type of limbo looking down on the world they've left behind. While we see this as a form of torment, they pass the time by messing with the minds of our children."

I then said, "I'm not sure I understand."

So she continued, "When this 'element' of society are still alive, they are monitored by our laws and justice system. But up there, they don't report to anyone and they in fact have a lot more fun because no one down here can see what they are doing."

I couldn't believe I was having this type of conversation with another human being. I certainly felt caught between two worlds. If anyone had been listening in to our conversation, I'm sure they would have thought we had both lost our minds. This was real, but I needed more clarification so I prompted her to continue.

"Over the past 3 days, I have talked to these 3 boys at great length! That's what they are after all; naughty boys! I explained to them that there is a better place for them. It's a place where they can do all the things they love and miss about being on earth. Things like skateboarding, BMX racing, football and swimming. I explained that when they undertake one of these activities, the supervisor they meet will be their spiritual teacher. One they can relate to, have fun with and learn from. You see they figured 'going toward the light' wasn't an option. It sounded completely ridiculous to sit under a light for the rest of their days, when being mischievous and messing with children's heads was much more entertaining. They now understand and they won't be back."

I felt completely drained and strangely energised all at the same time. Until now I'd felt like James and I had been living in a bubble; just us against the world. That bubble had now burst and we could re-join the world.

I asked Jaqueline what I should do next and she replied, "Just keep him home, love him and nurture him. You will know when the time is right to contact the school again. Kids live life in the moment, so don't worry, once he gets back he will make friends and settle in again."

The next day, peace had been restored to our home. To me, it felt like all the windows were open and a beautiful refreshing summer breeze had swept all the bad energy out of the house, never to return. The energy in our house felt incredibly different. Words can't describe it. I was thankful that it was something we all felt, even if some in the house didn't understand why.

The first day after the intense phone call from Jaqueline was spent quietly. The kitchen smelt like cupcakes and both James and our daughter spent most of the day playing nicely together. I couldn't help but just sit and watch them enjoy each other's company without fighting. It was heart-warming beyond belief. I began to wonder how I could ever thank Jaqueline for giving me back my son.

That night, my husband and I were doing the washing up at the kitchen sink. Our kids were sitting at their little bright yellow table and chairs colouring in together. They had been colouring in for nearly 3 hours. I was mesmerised. Neither of them had moved. This was a scene that I hadn't seen in months!

James actually looked like a different child. Actually, he looked like himself again and I found myself looking at him in a new light. Was that light coming from him? I don't know, but I loved it.

With tears in my eyes, I looked at my husband, the sceptic and said, "Look at them both enjoying themselves.

When's the last time you saw that? You can't deny what has happened here. You can't ignore the change." He said nothing, but I know he saw it.

If ever I was able to show a sceptic that there is more to life than this would have been the perfect opportunity.

Instead, he kept me grounded and for that I'm thankful.

James slept really well that night and every night after that.

The following day, I saw that James was considering throwing one of his normal tantrums but for some reason it didn't work for him! I clearly remember seeing him look over his shoulder as if looking for back up. He sensed that it wasn't there. Shrugged his shoulders and continued on his merry little way instead.

He never saw me watching him with tears rolling down my face! We never, ever saw any hint or sign of that mighty behaviour again.

Peace had been restored to our home.

Every day, I felt like I was unwrapping a very special present for the first time! James was so at peace. He was relaxed. He was spending quality time with his sister He was enjoying himself. She was enjoying herself in his company, no longer threatened or needing to be on guard around him. They were enjoying themselves.

By this time, James had had three and a half months off school and I from work.

It was time to ring the School.

What was I to say? Imagine for a moment, that this

was a situation you were in. How do you explain this to the Principal of a Catholic primary school?

Simply put, you don't!

I simply advised the Principal that I believed that James was ready to return to school if they would have him. I had to play the game. I should have changed schools! This is the one regret I have in my life.

The Principal told me that he would hold a meeting with the Deputy Principal, James' teacher and the school's counsellor and get back to me. Which they did, a couple of days later.

It was agreed that James could go back to school two days a week on a trial basis.

When he returned to school, James was sent home each day with a progress note from his teacher. I still have those notes today. In a nutshell, James' teacher was really enjoying having him in her classroom and stated that he was making a positive input into the activities and making friends as well. She too remarked that the behaviour displayed by James prior to the expulsion from school was nowhere in sight and as a result, agreed that he could come back to school full time.

Over the next few weeks and months, peace was restored in our home and in James' classroom. A little while later we attended an Open Night at the school. All the classrooms were open displaying the students work. We both knew it was going to be hard to explain James's change, so when we saw the principal coming, I cringed.

"Ah, Mr and Mrs Weatherburn. I just wanted to come

over and tell you what a wonderful job I think you have done as parents. James is settling in beautifully and I have had nothing but good reports from his teacher. Please tell me what kind of medication you have James on, as it's working wonderfully!"

Again, I cringed. I'm pretty sure my husband did too.

I was speechless. I really couldn't think of a response so I merely said, "Thanks." Before I needed to find a response, my husband grabbed my elbow and said, "Sorry, but I think our daughter over there wants us to look at a picture of hers on the wall. Thank you."

And just like that, that chapter of our life was over.

The Lesson

Every now and again, my attention is drawn to a current affairs programme on TV featuring allegedly naughty children. These children have been painted with the ADD / ADHD brush. Maybe 8 out of 10 children genuinely do have the disorder. However, I certainly feel that the other 2 are being tormented by entities like my son was. Or it may be that they are psychic themselves and the bad behaviour they demonstrate doesn't actually belong to them but to those around them.

Jacqueline explained to me that many children are misdiagnosed with ADD or ADHD. They are unnecessarily put on medication that may have detrimental side effects. All I ask is that parents consider what I've outlined here. It might save you years of pain.

Annie: A Desperate Mum's Plea

Dedicated to Steve, Melanie and Annie.

Sometimes I am put in positions where I am just so humbled by the power of the human spirit that I can only agree to play my part in someone else's story. This is what I have come to know as a 'starfish moment'. Such was the story of Steve, Melanie and Annie.

The death of a child from natural causes would have to be one of the most painful situations a parent can ever go through. I simply cannot imagine the grief and torment associated. No parent should ever have to bury their child.

The death of a child resulting from that child taking a heroin overdose would therefore have to result in unfathomable pain for the parents. Pain they must endure as they live the rest of their lives without their precious child.

I imagine that I too could be very tempted to want to join my child in death if this happened to me. I'd want to help them through the pain that pushed them to the point of wanting to end their life. This is how I met Annie, a mother going through the enormous loss of her youngest child due to a heroin overdose.

I had been working with Melanie, Annie's daughter, for a few months. We had had a few light discussions about my gift. Nothing too deep, but it had obviously been enough for Melanie to call me days after her 18 year old brother Steve's funeral. It was a cry for help like none I had ever seen before. Or for that matter, ever want to hear again.

I was riveted to a programme on TV when the incessant ring of the phone demanded that I answer it. Normally when home, I leave it to the answering machine to accept my calls. But I chose to answer. It was Melanie and she was hysterical.

"Marion, I need you. Please come and see my Mum for me. Please say you will come. Mum wants to take her own life so she can be with Steve."

I had never ever been in a situation like this before.

"I can't," I told her. "It's not my place. I wouldn't know what to say or do for your Mum."

"Please Marion, Mum and I have talked about your gift in the past. I know you can help her, I just know you can. No one else can. Please say you'll come."

In my head I began to think, "What could I possibly say that would change the mind of a woman so immersed in her own grief and determination to take her own life to be with her son?" I didn't see it as my place.

Melanie's mum was in a very personal space that no one could possibly enter. A very private place. I had never met

ANNIE: A DESPERATE MUM'S PLEA

Melanie's mum and certainly could not possibly enter that very private place in a grieving mother's heart. But Melanie was insistent. I could hear how scared she was of losing another family member, so I agreed to see her straight away.

I invited my Team and the archangels to come with me. I didn't know what to expect when I got there. I had to trust that the Universe had orchestrated this as one of those very special moments. And it was.

Melanie greeted me at the door and introduced me to her Mum, Annie. I have never ever been so close to personal pain and loss before. Annie's face that night will forever be permanently etched in my mind. Once beautiful eye, now empty.

Annie didn't speak, so I asked my guides to meet with Annie's. I was taken over and guided her to take my hand. All I could do was smile and held out my hand, which Annie took gratefully. I led Annie outside where we sat and held hands.

"Please," I begged my Team, "Give me something to say to help this poor woman." I had no words of my own. My Team had brought me here and I trusted them. I knew they would bring me the words to comfort Annie.

Annie was waiting. Waiting for a miracle, I think. Suddenly the pictures came to me.

"Annie, I am seeing Steve's coffin at the front of the school church. The church is filled with students, all with their head down. Outside the church, I see students standing huddled in groups, all with their heads down. I see students on the school oval and in classrooms all quietly focussed on the funeral taking place in their school chapel. I see teenagers standing in the suburbs all with their heads down. I see teenagers standing all over Australia and the world, all with their heads down, all thinking the same thing 'If this can happen to Steve, it can happen to me'. Annie, I sense that Steve's passing has touched the lives of many teenagers who also dabble in drugs. Steve's passing has caused a ripple affect amongst youth. I believe that with his passing, he has in fact saved the lives of many others who will now stop taking drugs. I believe the ripple effect was in place here. Your loss is a gift for others."

The profound visions then left me. We sat a moment in silence and then Annie said, "Wow. Thank you."

The silence continued, only now more comfortable. I did not have to wait long before the next vision came, this time with a very profound personal message for Annie.

What came next was the most beautiful moment I had ever experienced.

"Annie, I see a lady sitting on the edge of a bed throwing a tennis ball up and down in the air. She looks quite matronly."

I asked our guest who she was and whether she knew Annie. She said that her name was Melba. Melba was sitting on the edge of a bed covered in white sheets. When I looked at the head of the bed, I saw a young 18 year old male sleeping. Melba motioned to him and said, "That's Steve, I'm looking after him."

I asked Melba how she knew Annie to which she replied, "I used to live next door to Annie when the kids were young. I never married and never had kids. Whenever Annie's kids used to throw the tennis balls over the fence, I never returned them. Whilst she spoke, Melba continued to throw the tennis ball up in the air.

"Please tell Anita that whilst I never looked after her kids whenever she asked me to babysit, I will certainly be very happy to look after her son now. But most importantly, please tell Annie that if she does want to take her own life, she WILL NOT and I insist WILL NOT be reunited with Steve until the end of what would have been their natural lives. She will end up in limbo until then and will be more tormented than she is now as she will have to watch the rest of her family suffer without her. She will wish she was with them. Also, once the term of her natural life is up, she will need to be reborn to learn the lessons she never finished before taking her own life and this time the lessons will be even harder."

I suddenly realised that I needed to explain my vision to Annie. What would she say? How could I tell her what I saw? What if it wasn't real? I need not have worried. I told Annie everything from start to finish. Once done, I turned to Annie and the look on her face was one of absolute astonishment and delight.

"Yes, yes!" she exclaimed, "Perfect! How Perfect! Yes, Melba was my next-door neighbour. She was a spinster and yes she always kept the kids tennis balls, she must have hundreds of them as she would never give them back."

Was I imagining this? Annie had just confirmed for me that everything I told her about Melba was true. Yes, she had been her neighbour and had never married or had kids. She also never babysat for Annie even when Annie was desperate. Annie laughed when I explained that Melba kept tossing a tennis ball up and down in the air. She confirmed that that was exactly what she was like. She would never give back the kids balls when they went over the fence. Now we know why.

I just could not believe what was happening. This was very surreal and very special indeed.

It is vitally important that I add at this point that all of the information coming through me up to that point was coming through with the most amazing feeling of unconditional love and a feeling of incredible trust and respect. To be honest, there are no words that can describe what Annie and I experienced that night. It was simply amazing.

When I retell stories to people I sit with, I tend to focus on the person I am dealing with in the spirit world and once I have finished, I turn to look at the person I am Reading for.

Annie proceeded to ask me to thank Melba for sitting with her son until she could be reunited with him and for the amazing spiritual lesson around suicide. Annie told me that she was exhausted and wished to go inside to sleep.

We held hands at arm's length and stared into each other's eyes. Annie's soul had returned to her eyes. She was now at peace and had received a great deal of comfort and closure that night.

Me? I didn't sleep that night. I relived the whole experience repeatedly in my mind. I had left my house earlier in the night full of trepidation and fear. I came home at the end of night filled with awe at the power of unconditional love and proof that there is in fact life after death. Of that, I have never been more certain.

The Lesson

Well, firstly, I would like to say that I personally learnt a spiritual lesson so deep that night that it has kept me from taking my own life during times of deep, dark depression. We are given a set of spiritual lessons to learn here in this life. We need to tick those boxes before our souls can move to the next level. There are no shortcuts.

Lessons are presented to us repeatedly in this life. You may have noticed that they get bigger every time. You may find yourself asking questions like, "Why do these things keep happening to me?"

Next time you ask yourself this question, stop for a moment. Take stock and ask yourself, "What is the spiritual lesson here that I might need to learn?" If you think there isn't one and choose to respond with, "It's their fault," or, "They're this or that," you are mistaken. It's exactly when we say things like that that we need to realise it's really about us. Generally, the very thing you are blaming someone else for is really something you need to work on within yourself.

The sooner you learn the lesson that keeps presenting itself, the sooner you can get on with enjoying your life.

CAUGHT BETWEEN TWO WORLDS

The lesson here about suicide therefore, is that trying to take the shortcut out of our pain won't work. Melba has taught us this.

Over the years, I would run into Annie at the shops. Every time she saw me she would go out of her way to give me a hug and say a quiet thank you in my ear, before walking away to continue with her shopping and her life.

Do you know anyone at all that is very depressed, to the point of considering taking their own lives? Please let them know that there is no short cut to heaven, share this story with them and encourage them to get help.

Testimonial from Melanie

I asked Marion to come and sit with my Mum, who wanted to commit suicide to be with my brother who had recently lost his life to heroin. Reluctantly initially, Marion came to sit with my Mum and because of her explaining what would have happened to her if she had taken her own life, I have my Mum today.

Mum and I also had a fantastic message from our old neighbour Melba, whose name Marion knew. Marion saw Melba sitting on the edge of my brother's bed throwing a tennis ball in the air repeatedly whilst my brother rested on the other side. On querying how Melba knew my Mum, she laughingly replied, "I was her next door neighbour for many years. I never married and I never had or liked children (all the while throwing the tennis ball up in the air) and I never threw her kids tennis balls back over the fence when they landed there. I will now look after Steve until it's her turn to take over."

Renee: To Read or Not To Read

Dedicated to Renee and Robert

I've always read people before they arrived for their appointment with me. Many years ago my two best friends, Nairina and Jennifer, encouraged me to advertise in the local spiritual Newspaper in Perth, *Nova*, which is known elsewhere around Australia as *InnerSelf*. I now write for *InnerSelf* in South Australia from time to time. My friends knew from firsthand experience that people would answer my ad for Psychic Readings. They also knew that I needed to work in this field. They knew I would gain confidence to go on to help many people turn their lives around. Smart friends I had, and still have. So, I placed the ad.

I received a phone call during the week from a lady named Renee who asked for an appointment the following Saturday. We agreed to a time of 3pm, and I gave her my address.

At 2pm that Saturday, I sat in the garden with my

RENEE: TO READ OR NOT TO READ

pen and the special parchment paper that I used to write Readings on for people so they could take them home. I then watched Renee's 'DVD' in my mind. Rewinding, fast forwarding, pausing. Noting characters. Incidents. All the while, writing furiously as the information flooded onto the page.

It wasn't until I read my notes at the end that I realised something very profound had come through. I only hoped that what I was about to tell this lady was going to be true, otherwise I would look like a complete fool!

I prayed to my angels silently to sit with me whilst I walked Renee through her Reading. The following is an exact recount of Renee's Reading that sunny Saturday afternoon in the spring of 1997. Imagine you were on the receiving end of this Reading, how would you feel?

I knew this Reading was going to be intense. Was it doubt that I was feeling? Did I need reassurance that I did in fact have a Gift that I needed to share? There was the doorbell, here goes.

I opened the door to a petite and quietly spoken young lady aged about 28 years. I immediately liked her. We chatted whilst sitting at the kitchen table with a cuppa. I placed the scrolled paper Reading that I'd received earlier in front of her on the table. She didn't notice.

Renee started off by asking, "Would you like me to tell you why I'm here?" to which I replied, "No, please let me go first." I liked to go first, that way I had the proof that what I was doing was indeed real.

I began by explaining to Renee that I already knew why

she was coming to see me as I'd received her Reading earlier. I explained the way I received information. "Renee," I said, "You are here today because you are very keen to go back to part time work as a nurse. However, you are very worried about your 3 year old son who you need to put into day care. You are also worried about what your ex-mother-in-law thinks about it. Is that correct?" I asked.

Renee replied vehemently, "Oh yes, that's exactly why I'm here!" So I explained to her that returning to work was the best thing she could do at that moment in time. Her son would thrive in day care. As for the ex-mother-in-law, I explained that that's exactly what she is, the ex. The universe blesses your decision to go back to work, I told her.

"Thank you! But how did you know? I didn't tell you on the phone did I?"

"No you didn't, but you did come to me for psychic guidance and that's exactly what you've received."

Renee stood up as if to leave thinking she'd received what she'd come for. I asked her to sit down again as I was about to give her the most important, but unexpected news of the afternoon. She sat opposite me.

"Renee, whilst I was writing your Reading in the garden today, I received a visit from a lovely guy named Robert. Robert had red curly hair and freckles. He showed me a gun! A very distinct gun. It had a large brown barrel and an ivory handle with a horse carved into to it."

I was describing the gun with my hands in the space between us and just as I described the ivory handle, I saw silent tears rolling down Renee's face. Then with Robert's encouragement, I went on.

"Renee, Robert told me that he had not checked the gun before he cleaned it. It hadn't been used in ages, but cleaned it thoughtlessly. It was loaded. It killed him with the one and only bullet left in the barrel. Robert said that you, Renee, were and still are the only person that believed an accident had taken his life."

At this Renee was no longer the quiet, petite lady I'd met at the door earlier. She leapt up from her seat and proclaimed loudly, "I KNEW IT! I KNEW IT WAS AN ACCIDENT!!! EVEN HIS MOTHER STOOD UP AT THE FRONT OF HIS COFFIN AT THE FUNERAL BERATING HIM FOR BRINGING SUCH ANGUISH AND DESPAIR TO HER FAMILY! I knew. I knew," she repeated the words through tears.

I was covered in goose bumps.

Renee sat back down with a look of absolute shock and disbelief on her face. This was not after all, what she'd come here for today! Robert had recounted the exact same scenario about his Mother at the funeral earlier in the garden and here was Renee confirming it. Robert then took over the rest of the conversation through me to Renee.

It was extraordinary.

He told Renee that they had always been the best of friends. Not lovers, not even boyfriend and girlfriend, just really good friends. Robert reassured Renee that he remained her best friend today and all she ever need do is think of him and he'll be right there by her side as her guide. Not many of us get to meet our guides like Renee did.

Robert asked me to place Renee's hand on the seat beside her so he could hold it. I asked her to do this. I thought she may not...but she did. Very gingerly, Renee placed her hand where I asked her to and when I saw Robert place his hand over hers, Renee visibly flinched and said, "Oh my! I think I just felt him! Could I have?"

I was in awe. Everything I'd received an hour before Renee arrived was true, real and confirmed as fact by all of Renee's expressions and tears.

After 25 minutes, Renee sighed and looked at me with a very peaceful look and said, "Marion, may I give you a hug please? I never hug anyone, but today you have given me something I never thought I would get in my life – closure. For the loss of my best friend. More than that, you've given me back my best friend, how can I ever thank you? I came here today simply to get reassurance that my 3 year old son would be ok in day care whilst I went back to a job I loved. You gave me the approval I was seeking and so much more. I just wish I'd taped this conversation as it's simply unbelievable."

To which I replied, "Renee, its ok." I pointed to the Reading tied with a white ribbon in front of her. "There's your Reading. Word for word as I received it from Robert this afternoon."

Renee asked me how much I charged and I told her that I didn't accept payment. We hugged and she left. Both of us were different people for the experience we shared that day. I didn't sleep that night. I relived Renee's Reading and Robert's visit over and over in my mind. Was it real? It certainly was.

The Lesson

What can we learn from Renee's Reading and Robert's visit? Renee was hoping that her Reading would give her the confirmation she was seeking to go back to work. Her request was simple. She received both the facts and the permission.

These types of Readings are what I call Readings of and for the Physical World and the Physical Self. Often we seek guidance to help us get through everyday life when we just can't seem to make a decision for ourselves. We need a Psychic to show us our options and if we're lucky, to define a clear path and direction.

People who seek Readings like this have never really learnt to trust their own intuition. Intuition is more commonly known as 'having a hunch' or a 'gut feel' and we've all experienced that. We can all think of a time when we've had a hunch and chosen to ignore it. I bet you can, and I bet you lived to regret it too. Maybe after a Melbourne Cup race! But still you repeatedly ignored it.

These hunches will recur over and over until you've learnt to trust that gut instinct or hunch and deal with it head on. We've all been blessed with the gift of intuition. You don't need to visit a Psychic Medium for that kind of information.

What you need to go to a Psychic Medium for is the

other half of Renee's Reading. In hope that you too will receive a visit from a very special friend who has been following you all your life. When you finally get to a place where they can contact you, they will.

That's a real Reading and that's why I always capitalise the first letter of the word Reading. I encourage you to experience the difference for yourself.

Can your rational mind possibly accept that death only separates us temporarily from those we love and that if our loved ones really want to contact us they will? It's up to us then to listen, really listen.

Testimonial from Renee

I saw Marion for a Reading about whether or not I should return to work and put my son in day care. I was in two minds as he was so young and I was a single mum.

Marion reassured me that this was the right thing to do for both of us. I returned to work and have enjoyed several promotions over the years. I have my confidence back. However, what I also received was some very surprising information about a very special person that had passed many years ago. Marion was able to give me my friends' name and full description of his features including how he died. I thought I had lost that dear friend of mine but thanks to Marion bringing him through for me, I have received great comfort and closure to many questions that were still burning for me and I now have him as my close friend again! Awesome Marion! Just awesome!

Sophie: Secret Lover Surprise

Dedicated to Sophie and Peter

I first started advertising my Psychic services way back in 1997, still as a hobby. When someone phoned me for an appointment, I only gave them a time, date and my address. Sophie came to see me one Saturday in 1998. For the first 45-50 minutes, I got absolutely nothing. I refuse to ask my clients any questions. But given that nothing was coming through, I told Sophie that I was obviously a fraud and apologised for taking her time that morning.

She said it was fine and intimated that she wanted to keep talking. So we chatted about meaningless stuff like her matching necklace, earrings, shoes and handbag. That was the extent of our conversation. I was so very uncomfortable and embarrassed. The awkwardness between us was tangible.

In my head I was swearing I'd never do this again as long as I lived. Clearly, I couldn't do it. I really didn't know how to ask Sophie to leave and I was feeling quite awkward for both of us. Then, out of nowhere, in my mind's eye I saw a man aged approximately 32. He smiled at me.

Suddenly with an overwhelming feeling of love, I knew we had a connection for Sophie. She saw my face change as I strained to make contact with her guest. She said, "Marion, you've got something. Whatever it is, tell me."

I put my hand up to quieten her and asked her guest to introduce himself to me. A gorgeous man with dark curly hair, dark eyebrows and eyelashes with the most gorgeous 'come to bed' eyes that I've ever seen introduced himself to me as Peter. I silently hoped he was there for me. Then I realised that that would be fruitless, considering he was dead!

I asked Peter if he knew Sophie. Peter said, "Yes I know Sophie."

So I asked, "How do you know Sophie and do you have a message for her?"

Peter replied, "I have been following Sophie around until she found someone like you who could give her a message for me."

"Ok, go on, what is your message? I will tell her," I said.

"Tell Sophie I love her, always have and always will."

"Peter, that's a wonderful message, however, you need to give me more than that. Something more personal please."

Sophie interjected here and asked, "What's happening Marion, you have to tell me, even if it's bad."

I continued to listen to Peter, "Ask Sophie about the night before her wedding when she spent the night with me and married the wrong guy the next day."

SOPHIE: SECRET LOVER SURPRISE

My jaw must have dropped six inches in shock. "WHAT?" I exclaimed out loud.

"WHAT?" screeched Sophie.

Peter simply said, "Go on, ask her, you'll see. She needs to know I'm here."

At this point I need to add that an incredible doubt had crept in. I felt that there was no way this could be real. I feared Sophie might slap me when I gave her that message. But Peter guided me to tell her his message.

So I plucked up the courage, "Sophie, I have this gorgeous guy here with you who gave me his name as Peter. Peter has dark hair, dark eyelashes and big dark brown eyes. He's aged approximately 32 and he's absolutely gorgeous."

When I have a guest with me as well as the client, I look at neither of them to ensure I hear and see clarity of information. I look between them when relaying messages.

"Peter has asked me to ask you about the night before your wedding, the night you spent with him. Before marrying the wrong guy the next day."

All the while I was thinking to myself, "What if I'm making this up. I do after all have a vivid imagination. What if I'm way off track? How humiliating. Yet, the feeling of intense love that Peter brought with him reassured me that it was safe to give Sophie his message. My next glance at Sophie confirmed that Peter was in fact here with us both as Sophie had tears streaming down her cheeks.

She said, "Marion, NO-ONE knew where I was the night before my wedding! No-one! Yes, I really did marry the wrong guy and I've regretted it ever since."

Sophie suddenly realised that Peter must surely have passed away in order for his Spirit to communicate with us.

"Is he dead? Has Peter died?" Sophie cried.

I asked Peter, "Are you dead?"

Peter said, "No."

"He says no, Sophie," I was excited now. I looked back at Peter and said, "Well, how does that work then?"

He replied, "We are all energy. Love is an energy. I loved Sophie more than anyone else and needed her to know. People who have passed have energy. People alive have energy. If you really love or have loved someone so intensely during your life you will find a way to make contact with them."

Peter and I sat in silence for a while as Sophie wept for a lost love. Before long she turned to me and smiled and said, "I'm glad I stayed. Thank you. This was not what I expected from a Reading, but it is the best gift you could have given me. Thank you."

I sat in silent shock for the next few hours, coming to terms with all that had happened. For me it remains a miracle to have this kind of very real contact and confirmation. I do not take it for granted. It is a privilege. It is real.

The Lesson

Before Facebook, email and even mobile phones, there was no real way to keep in touch to know how things were

SOPHIE: SECRET LOVER SURPRISE

going for a client after they had had a Reading. There was also never a reason to know.

Peter's gift to me was a very special one. Up until Sophie's Reading, I had only ever had contact with the Souls and Spirits of people that had passed over. Peter was, in fact, still alive. He loved Sophie so much and had followed her around until she came to someone like me so he could give her his important message.

Peter explained to me that we are all energy whether alive in this life or the next life. He also showed me that as Psychic Mediums we cannot just ring the doorbell above the clouds and summon forward the Soul of a person passed over just because the person who has come for the Reading wants to make contact. This is just impossible. All the famous Mediums out there like John Edwards, James Van Praagh and Alison Dubois state vehemently that this is simply not possible. Be very wary of anyone who claims they can do this. It simply does not work this way.

We all believe that any Spirit, whether alive in this life or next, will come through to you if they want to or if you need to hear a very important spiritual message. Expect the Unexpected when you come for a Reading.

Did you know that you do not need to visit a Psychic or Medium in order to make contact with a loved one that has passed over? Light some candles, put on some lovely music, get comfy with a nanny rug and simply sit. Leave your ego outside the room and come right into your Soul.

Fill your heart and soul with love and peace. This is not a circus trick, this is real. Close your eyes, imagine your loved one in your mind's eye, and talk to them. Simply talk. Ask them questions. Try it for yourself. If they do not come through straight away you may be visited in your dreams that night or the next as Spirits feel more comfortable coming through in a way that your rational mind can deal with. You might just be pleasantly surprised.

Testimonial from Sophie

I didn't know what to expect when I came to see Marion for a Reading in 1998. I got way more than I bargained for, but appreciated hearing that the man I spent the night with before the day I married my husband was in fact the man I should have married. At the time, I felt that I was marrying the wrong man. But now I'm now a dedicated wife and mother to two beautiful girls.

No-one knew this about me. No one knew where I was the night before my wedding, that I'd dared to risk everything for one last night with the man I loved more than the man I was to marry the next day. Why did I go through with the marriage? To this day I don't know and it is a regret I have to live with but I will carry Peter's love in my heart forever.

Heather: How Do You Know You're Dead?

Dedicated to Heather and her Dad

I greeted Heather at my door on a Saturday afternoon in 1987. She was a very graceful, well-coiffed woman aged in her mid60's. But boy was she flustered! After settling her down with a pot of tea and matching cup and saucer, I asked Heather why she came to see me.

"Well, I just cannot put my finger on it," she said. "I am all at sea with my emotions. My moods are all over the shop. This just is not like me. I feel so restless. I start one job, then another before finishing the first. I was hoping you might be able to give me some healing or something."

Whilst Heather was talking, I saw an older man in my vision. White hair, mostly on one side of his head and a very prominent red birthmark on the left hand side of his face. He was wearing only a white sheet wrapped around his middle. He too seemed flustered. I was trying to focus on Heather but was becoming quite distracted by this vision.

I put my hand up to Heather to let her know I was getting something. I had joined the man in the vision. Together we were walking in silence, hand in hand through a forest of trees playfully lit by the late afternoon sun. The air was warm.

I turned and asked Heather if her Father had recently passed, and described the man in my vision. She squealed a little girly squeal and confirmed that I had indeed described her Dad who had died about 3 months before.

I asked Heather how long she had been feeling the way she did, "Well, actually ever since my Dad died to be honest."

I went back to the vision. The man and I were walking towards a very sunlit circle in the forest. In the middle, there was bed. It looked like a hospital bed. The bed was covered in a white sheet. There seemed to be a body underneath it. We walked to the side of the bed. I gently pulled back the covers to reveal the same man who was standing next to me.

"Oh," he exclaimed, "Now, I get it! I'm dead! I couldn't work out what was wrong with me and why Heather was ignoring me. I thought I'd upset her! I know exactly what to do now." And with a wink he was gone!

I looked back at Heather and told her everything that I had just seen. Heather shook her head and heavy tears fell onto her lap. "That makes so much sense," she said, "Thank you."

Heather and I chatted further a while longer before she left.

HEATHER: HOW DO YOU KNOW YOU'RE DEAD?

I answered a knock on the door a few weeks later and was greeted by a big bunch of flowers, Heather peeking out from behind them.

Heather told me that ever since the day she met with me, she had improved daily and was finally feeling at peace and herself again.

The Lesson

When a loved one passes away suddenly, they pass over so quickly that sometimes they don't realise what has happened to them and that's why you can feel them around you. They are used to being around you and that's where they feel comfortable. Sometimes they choose to stay around you because the grief you are experiencing saddens them too and they try to reach out to console you. This is why you may see them at the end of your bed during the night or smell their perfume or after shave, or hear their favourite music over and over.

If you do sense them, be sure to let them know how much they mean to you. Never ever be fearful that you will lose them permanently. Life on earth is only temporary. In the next life, we are with them for eternity. Let them know that you give them permission to move onto the next chapter in their Book of Life and that you will hold them in your hearts until you are together again.

Cazz: Pennies From Heaven

Dedicated to Cazz and her family

Cazz's Reading was one of those Readings that make me feel truly blessed. I received a phone call one day from a lovely woman named Cazz who had an extremely strong Irish accent. My Team told me that Cazz had something very special to share with me. They were right.

She said that she had felt compelled to ring me as I kept appearing on her Facebook news feed. "What exactly do you do and why am I drawn to ring you?" she asked straight out, "I never do things like that. Ring strangers I mean. But I was compelled to ring you. What exactly do you do?"

I gave Cazz an overview of the work that I do explaining that I work at a very deep Soul level. I offer spiritual guidance and direction from both my own Team and those of the person I am Reading for. "Souls are quite simple," I explained. "Souls just want to love and be loved. Humans complicate their lives with their egos and attitudes. A good percentage of people are way off their spiritual paths. If they find a way back to their path, their lives flow much easier. Humans complicate their lives with attitude, envy, competitiveness, materialism, negativity, anger and jealousy. My job is to help you back on the path."

"I'm a sceptic," Cazz said, "I don't know why I've rung you."

I explained to Cazz that there is a difference between receiving psychic messages for the sake of it and receiving messages delivered with guidance, clarity and direction. I said that the latter is what I do. She then explained that she had been raised a strict Irish Catholic and had moved to Australia two years earlier. She told me that she believed in God, Heaven and Hell and that anything remotely superstitious was linked to the devil and not to be explored. Séance's were evil and for anyone who may have been possessed by an evil Spirit, a Priest was called to perform an exorcism and clear the house. She was clearly a sceptic.

Cazz went onto say that she also believed in Angels, coincidences and that everything happened for a reason. But these were new feelings to her. She then thanked me for my time and ended the phone call.

An hour later, she rang me back and asked if I could possibly see her the next day. As luck would have it, I had had a cancellation and it suited Cazz's timing perfectly.

The next day, I greeted a very nervous Cazz at the door. I made a cuppa and we both snuggled up on the lounge suites with our nanny rugs, cuppa and blackcurrant jubes. We continued our conversation from where we'd left it the day before. She was hungry to know more and asked some very good questions.

It's interesting when people start asking questions, because spirits usually answer them for me and we both end up learning from the discussion.

I still felt that Cazz had something very special to talk to me about and so I asked her about it. "Cazz, I get the sense that despite your strong religious upbringing, you have had something very significant happen to you in your life. I feel that it is what brought you here today and I would love to hear about it."

The light was fading fast outside and the warm glow from the candles certainly set the mood for what Cazz was about to tell me. A real sense of love filled the room. Cazz, held my gaze, took a deep breath and began.

"Four years ago in Ireland, my husband and I had been trying to have a baby. After years of trying naturally, we fell pregnant using the IVF method of fertilisation. We were over the moon. Just four weeks into the pregnancy, I lost the baby. My husband and I were devastated. I personally was shattered. My husband took me to Portugal for a break to help me heal emotionally. One particular day, we were walking the streets, shadows of ourselves. Both completely absorbed in our own grief and feelings. It was raining. We kept walking. The sky was crying with us. We felt so alone. Suddenly we heard a tinkle on the ground. Something hard had fallen to the ground. My husband bent down and picked up a golden coin. We looked at it together. On one side, it had a picture of an Angel. On the other side was the inscription 'For the New Mother.'"

Both Cazz and I were weeping openly now. This was in fact a miracle. A real miracle. Cazz said that she believed that penny had been sent from Heaven to let her know that everything would be ok and that she would have a baby one day. She said that she still has that penny and will never ever let it out of her sight. It is her proof that miracles really do happen to everyday people, right when they need them.

The Lesson

We hope and pray for miracles every day. But are they really the ones we need? If your prayers for a miracle are not being answered, I would recommend that you look at what it is exactly you are asking for.

Cazz's miracle was a very personal one. One that provided amazing healing and restoration of faith in life itself. It inspired Cazz and her husband to keep going. Miracles are sacred and really do happen when you least expect them. Cazz and her husband have had another miracle since then, the birth of their beautiful son.

Her story will stay in my heart forever and makes me truly thankful and aware that everyone out there has their own special story to share. My own faith was strengthened that day, it was exactly the miracle I needed.

Whilst I am my own biggest sceptic at times, Readings

like Cazz's confirm for me that we really know very little about life and just when we think we cannot take another step, we receive a miracle. Miracles are sent to reassure us that we are indeed blessed, even though during tough times we feel anything but. They cannot be commanded, demanded or requested. They are sent to those in need at exactly the right time. Without question. Without explanation. Without hesitation.

With love.

Testimonial from Cazz

Thank you for my reading Marion, it was so nice to meet you I hope the benefit of foresight you gave me will allow me enjoy my family so much more.

Helen: Silence Is Golden

Dedicated to Helen

It was a hot 42 degree November day when I met with Helen for a Reading in 2015. I was greeted with cool air-conditioning, a long cool refreshing drink and a very warm, friendly personality.

Helen and I chatted about the weather while I waited for Spirit to take over the Reading for us. But, alas. Today I had nothing. zilch, nix, nada, nothing at all!

I was confused and somewhat embarrassed. I pleaded with my Team to bring me through information to guide Helen in her life along with any messages from loved ones. But still, the silence was deafening.

So, what do I do in circumstances like this? Mix it up. Firstly I Read Helen's 17 year old daughter. As a highly intelligent and diligent student, I saw a future as a Vet. Helen confirmed that that was exactly what her daughter was studying towards and said that her daughter would be very pleased to hear the confirmation.

CAUGHT BETWEEN TWO WORLDS

Then I scanned Helen's 15 year old daughter. I got the sense that this girl excelled in recess and lunchtime and would be a career Mum rather than a professional. Helen told me that she got the same sense about her youngest daughter and that many times her daughter has said that just wanted to be a Mum when she grew up. Again, Helen said that her youngest daughter would be very pleased to hear this confirmation.

I was bewildered with the lack of information about Helen coming through. Maybe it was the heat. Maybe I really couldn't do it anymore. I decided to Read Helen's husband. All I got was that he was a very proud family man and very happily married. Helen's husband was secure in his job and within his relationship with Helen. Money was not an issue as they were comfortable and were always able to pay their bills on time. That was it.

I again pleaded with my Team to bring me through information to guide Helen in her life along with any messages from loved ones. Nothing.

I had no idea what was going on and I was becoming decidedly uncomfortable. I felt like a fraud. More conversation about the weather.

As I sat opposite Helen, I waited patiently for information that would redeem me from total embarrassment. "Helen," I said, "It must be the heat today as I'm really not getting any information or messages through for you today. I'm sorry."

I continued on to tell her that I felt her life was really on track and perhaps that was why I was not getting

HELEN: SILENCE IS GOLDEN

anything for her. I sensed that she was happily married and together with her husband, had raised two very sensible and intelligent teenage girls. I got the sense too that money would always come easily for them and they would never struggle.

Furthermore, I told Helen that the confrontations she had been going through with her best friend were just about over and reconciliation would soon start. I got the sense that there were no visitors from above the clouds today for Helen and again I apologised.

It is simply not possible to knock on Heaven's Door and expect it to be opened by the very people you may be hoping to hear from.

Despite mostly talking about the weather, ninety minutes had passed. I apologised to Helen that there were no messages that day from friends or family that had passed on and no spiritual guidance for her in her life as such. I told her that if anything came through now, I would be making it up and I never wanted to do that. I told her that I would leave and get myself some lunch before the next Reading. Helen's life, it seemed, was unremarkable. But Helen intercepted me, opening her purse to pay me.

"Oh no, I exclaimed. I haven't given you anything."

But to Helen, it was indeed remarkable!

Helen said to me, "But Marion! That is where you are wrong! You've given me EXACTLY what I needed today. You see, I know that everything's on track with my husband, daughters and myself. I do not have any relatives or friends that have passed over yet. I did not want any messages today. I wanted confirmation that my life is exactly as I thought it was."

And it was. The Reading was, as it turned out, perfect!

The Lesson

Why do people want a Psychic Reading? Some people want the lotto numbers, some want direction in their careers. Some people want the name of their future partner, some want clarity regarding issues in their relationships.

Others want guidance as to how to be the best parent they can be. Some want to know about their health or that of family members, others want closure after the passing of a loved one from this life into the next. Some people want proof of life after death to help them feel that their struggle is worthwhile.

But, some people just want to know that everything they are doing is just right. That's all Helen wanted. Confirmation.

Ted: Psychic Testing Underway

Dedicated to Ted

It happens so often. It feels like I am being scrupulously interviewed for a job. I'd like to question why people feel the need to test psychic ability. Is it about catching the Psychic out? Or is it about the Psychic catching them out?

Here is a true story about such an occasion where the sceptic put me, the Psychic, to the test and was gobsmacked when I passed the interview with flying colours!

My ex-husband used to work as a courier. He used to deliver to a business where a man named Ted worked. He delivered there every fortnight over a period of years. Over the years, a friendship had formed and the two discussed everything from motorbikes, camping and wives to their children.

Every now and again, my Psychic abilities would come up in conversation. Ted always said he was not a believer of such rubbish. Fair enough, I thought. I always knew that one day Ted would experience proof first hand. That day came in November 2010.

My husband and I went to a car rally where he introduced me to Ted and we began lunch. It was a most glorious day and hundreds of cars at the annual Big Al's Poker car run surrounded us. This was a car run for car enthusiasts around Perth and was patronised by over 400 cars.

When I was introduced to Ted, he said to me "Oh so you are the Psychic!" He went on to say, "I'd like to put you to the test. Are you up for it?"

I cringed. Here we go again, "Ok," I said.

Ed said to me, "I've got something in the glovebox of my car and I want you to tell me what it is by the end of today. Ok?" I gave no answer.

"Ok?" Ted asked again.

I had not answered him the first time as I was already fighting tears after the first "Ok?" I let the tears stream down my face because I knew exactly what he had in his glove box.

Ted asked me why I was crying. So did my husband. I told them that I already knew what Ted had in his glovebox and it made me feel very sad. His car was an old Blues Brothers style USA Police Car and was carrying around some very valuable cargo in its glovebox.

I knew that Ted was carrying around something of incredible sentimental value relating to his best friend. I also knew that his best friend had already passed over. I felt that Ted was carrying either his best friend's ashes or something relating to his funeral.

I could not stop the tears. Such was the intensity of the

TED: PYSCHIC TESTING UNDERWAY

friendship and sadness of their bond. I felt that Ted's best friend wanted to continue living life through Ted, who lived life large.

However, I said nothing. I did not see Ted again for the rest of the day. We enjoyed taking part in the famous Poker Run in our beautiful, sleek, left hand drive 1979 Corvette Stingray.

A friend asked me what it was that I thought Ted had in his glovebox. Again, I teared up. "What is it?" he prodded. I started by saying that I hoped I was wrong but that I sensed that he had something in his glovebox relating to the passing of his best friend and I hoped above hope that it wasn't his ashes and just something relating to the funeral.

Weaving our way through 400 cars, we arrived at the spot our friends had been holding for us. Ted was already there. Together we walked to the staging area and enjoyed a beer and the prize presentations. I felt a sense of impending doom. I knew Ted was going to test me as to the contents of his glovebox. Oh boy, I hated being tested. What if I was wrong? What if I was right?

At many times during my life, people have tested me in this way. However, this was the most profound test of them all. For all I knew, Ted could have a torch in his glovebox, a street directory or a packet of chewing gum. Surely not anything related to his best friend that had died?

I hoped I was wrong but part of me also knew that I was right. But how could I know? All I did was psychically look into his glovebox. Before I knew it, Ed was at our side. "So, have you worked out what was in my glovebox then Miss Psychic?"

I started to speak but could not as the tears were stuck in my throat. I motioned to my partner to answer on my behalf. "Ted, Marion felt straight away this morning that you were carrying something very special relating to your best friend. A friend who had passed away. She felt that you were either carrying his ashes or something relating to his passing or funeral and that's why she started crying this morning and is struggling now to talk to you about it because it feels so real."

Ted stopped dead in his tracks. Tears glistened in his eyes and everything became surreal. Even the light seemed different. He took my hand and as the tears slid down his face. He told me that I was right and that in fact he had the flyer from his best friend's funeral in his glove box together with a photo of him that he carried with him everywhere he went. His friend had always asked him to take him on any road trip that he did so that he could enjoy living larger than life, just like Ted did.

The Lesson

Why do people feel the need to test a Psychic? Is it because they want to prove themselves as sceptics to be right? Or is it because they are genuinely curious as to whether a Psychic can in fact do as they claim? Or are they curious as to whether their own lives will continue after they pass on? No answers for this one, just questions you should ask yourself.

Every Day Is Mother's Day

Dedicated to my mum, mums and mums-to-be everywhere

Magical
Unconditional
Miracle

Mums are magical. Their love is unconditional. Their patience, tolerance, compassion and creativity is nothing short of a miracle. That's a fact. We spend our teenage years avoiding our mums and it is not until we are mums ourselves that we really appreciate and understand everything they did and sacrificed for us. Only then do we appreciate them and miss them when we lose them.

Mums are the soft place to fall on during our lives; physically, emotionally and spiritually. For those of you who have already lost your mums, I know you miss their physical presence. By keeping their love in your heart, you never lose them. You are only apart until you are both together again when the time is right and your work here on earth is again done.

For those of you that still have your mum, please cherish each waking moment. Make it all count. Do not merely exist alongside them. Life goes by so very fast and too often we take our mums for granted, not appreciating what they have done for us in our lives until they have passed.

Back in 1997, I found myself at a gift store in a shopping centre in Perth. You know those card stands often located outside of gift stores and newsagents with birthday cards and the like. Well I was standing at one of those stands holding Mother's Day cards.

One card in particular caught my eye and I reached out for it. At the same time, another hand reached out next to me to the same card. Suddenly, I was guided by Spirit to place my hand on top of hers. In a very soothing, compassionate voice that was not my own, I said, "Your Mum knows how much you love her and miss her. She told me to tell you that you don't need to buy her a card this year."

The woman next to me dissolved into tears. She sobbed that her Mum had just died and it felt automatic to buy her a Mother's Day card. We stood in the shop doorway hugging and crying for about five minutes, oblivious to everyone walking into and out of the shop.

Then we stepped back, she held my hands and looked deep into my still glassy eyes and whispered, "Thank you. I don't know how you knew, but thank you." Then we both turned and walked away, changed forever, both whispering silent prayers of gratitude, thanks and love to our mums.

CAUGHT BETWEEN TWO WORLDS

I dedicate this story to all mums. Your job is one of the hardest in the world. It's only other mum's that understand all you go through to raise your family. Your job is one of the most fulfilling in the world. To me, being a mum to my beautiful daughter and amazing son is like unwrapping the most fantastic Christmas present each and every day of their lives.

I also dedicate this story also to all the amazingly awesome kids out there because without you, we would not get to experience the fabulous world of being a mum.

As a mum to my own two children, I often draw on my own experiences as a child, what I liked and what I didn't like about the way I was parented. I then adjust my own parenting styles to suit. Often, when talking to other mums, I find a common thread whereby we all seem to want to raise our own kids the way we wished we'd been raised. We always honour our own mums, who did the very best they could at the time. It's just that we like to do things differently.

I obviously believed it was vitally important for me to bring up my two kids to have a strong spiritual foundation. I feel that the following words of wisdom are the most important thing I taught my two: "Listen to your heart."

By the time my son had turned five, I was not sure what else I could do to discipline him whenever he tormented his sister. The naughty corner did not work, time out did not work, smacking did not work, and taking away his favourite toys did not work. I was getting desperate and had to find something that did work.

On one particularly trying day, my son had just taken my daughter's polar bear from her. That polar bear and her were joined at the hip. I'm reasonably sure she still sleeps with it to this day. She was sobbing uncontrollably. I was getting so tired and worn down by his behaviour.

I squatted down next to my son and looked him deep in the eye. I said to him, "Listen to your heart. Just listen to your heart and you will know what to do next." I walked away.

Peeking around the corner of the room, I saw my son give the polar bear back to his sister. To this day, I still advise both kids to listen to their hearts when they need to find an answer to a situation they are struggling with.

Listen to your heart turned out to be one of the only disciplines that actually worked. As a five year old, my son already understood the concept of listening to his inner voice.

When was the last time you told your mum how much she meant to you? When was the last time you told your mum about what you feel was the most important thing she ever taught you? When was the last time you talked to your mum about your most valuable memory of growing up? When was the last time you listened to your mum? What do you find yourself still doing today that your mum once taught you?

Evelyn & Emma: A Special Bond

Dedicated to Evelyn, Andrew and Emma

On the morning of Evelyn's Reading, my Team told me that I would experience something very special. When I checked my diary at 7am that morning, I saw Evelyn's name down in the afternoon. I thought to myself, "I'm sure Evelyn was booked in for this morning."

Then I got a message through from a lady named Shirley, who was connected to Evelyn. She said, "No love, she's booked in for this afternoon. Evelyn's coming this afternoon."

It was a lovely warm sunny day when I welcomed Evelyn to my home. I prepared afternoon tea complete with teapot, cups and saucers and biscuits. I liked Evelyn straight away. I liked Evelyn's husband Andrew straight away, too.

Turns out everybody loved Andrew straight away. It was a real shame that he had to pass so young. But just because he had passed from the physical world, didn't mean that he had left Evelyn's world. Andrew and Evelyn were joined at the hip. I could see that very clearly. They were very much in love.

Evelyn said that she always felt Andrew around her. She didn't just say the words, she meant it. She really did feel him in her life. I was able to describe Andrew to Evelyn very clearly. I also described their dog Boss. Boss and Andrew were best friends.

I asked Evelyn if Andrew used to be in the Country Fire Service (CFS) and whether she would be able to get his old helmet and keep it at home somewhere special. I asked her to put the helmet on the lounge suite so that Boss could be near his beloved owner.

Evelyn kept asking me if it was ok that Andrew stayed by her side. "Shouldn't he go to the light or something?" Evelyn asked me.

"Evelyn, your relationship with Andrew was very special and very blessed. Andrew's leaning right next to you. He knows you need him and miss him and he needs and misses you. You were both very much in love. You are his heaven and that's exactly where he is and wants to stay! Please don't rush him away."

Evelyn and I shared some very special tears that afternoon. She didn't want Andrew to go anywhere but she felt selfish that she wanted to keep him close to her. I reassured her that Andrew has made his choice and that he would wait for her at which point Andrew interrupted our conversation and told me to tell Evelyn to, "Take your time love, I'll be right here. No need for you to rush through your life just so we can be together again. Life goes fast enough. Enjoy it with the kids."

Evelyn and I chatted awhile about the amazing feeling of love that had accompanied her Reading so far. But then I started laughing! "Evelyn," I said. "I'm laughing because all I can see is you holding up a really big pair of trousers in front of you! I also have a lady's name, Shirley, for you. Shirley came through to me at 7am this morning. However, I sense that Shirley is still alive and she's saying that you will know exactly what to do with these trousers! She's also telling me now that she's very proud of who you have become and you were one of her favourite students. You listened well, learnt well and produced beautiful work. I see that she's giving you a gold star. Does any of this make any sense to you?"

Evelyn started laughing and crying at the same. "Where do I begin?" She said, "I'm a dressmaker and just this morning a really big man came in and asked me to find a way to make his trousers bigger and also shorter for him. He was such an unusual fit and I had no idea why he didn't just go and buy himself a new pair of trousers. It really seemed ridiculous to me. But you're right, Shirley was my dearest Sewing Teacher. She's still alive."

Evelyn stopped a moment to collect herself as the impact of Shirley's message hit home. She continued, "I would not be a Dressmaker with my own business if it hadn't been for Shirley. She was the most amazing teacher and taught me everything I know."

"Evelyn, I see an opportunity for you to give Shirley a bunch of flowers at a morning tea. I recommend that you buy a bunch of lovely flowers and a beautiful card, one that is blank. Please write in there a little letter to Shirley. Tell her the impact she has had on your life. This is one of the most important outcomes of today's Reading Evelyn! Shirley needs to read your heartfelt thoughts. It is going to go a long way to some healing for her. Nothing you need to worry about and she may be taken aback by the gesture, but trust me, on a spiritual level…it is a perfect gesture! You will work out when and where".

"Well, Shirley is part of a sewing group I am in that meets once a month."

Evelyn thought it sounded like a beautiful suggestion and that she would make the effort at the next sewing meeting.

Some weeks later, Evelyn's daughter Emma came to see me. I didn't realise she was Evelyn's daughter until much later in her Reading, when Andrew, also Emma's Dad, came through for her.

Once we were settled, I told Emma that I sensed a little girl around her (living) with the name Lee Lee. The name seemed unusual to me, but then again, the message is not for me to understand. Emma confirmed that her daughter's name was Lillias. She told me that she was a sceptic and that this was her first Reading and already she was enjoying the experience.

I asked Emma if she was thinking about moving and she told me that they had seen a house they wanted to put an offer on but were seeking confirmation from me as to whether they should. I recommended that they did not buy this house, because there was a house with the initials MB (Mount Barker or Murray Bridge) that was currently being prepared for sale and would suit them better.

I then asked Emma if they were considering having another baby? She initially said no quite vehemently. However when I explained that I felt that a baby boy was waiting for her to be ready, she considered the option. I said, "On behalf of your Dad, I would like to say that he would love your son to be named Andrew. In fact, he would be honoured!"

And with that the tears began to flow. For both of us. I took Emma's hand so that she could feel the most amazing feeling of love and protection that her Dad was showering us with.

I introduced psychometry to Emma to help her make her own decisions. I taught her how to Read the information that came through. I asked Emma if we could use her wedding ring as the object. After threading the ring with cotton, Emma's dad asked me to tell Emma that he saw that ring being put on her finger at her wedding and Yes! He was there that day!

Emma's Dad said, and I told her through my tears, that whilst she asked him for help, she didn't listen to his answers. So, he said, "When you ask the ring a question, ask it like this: 'Dad, show me a yes or no." He said that it would be him providing the answers for her. She now knew for certain that he was still being her Dad. I said, "You might not be able to see him but you can feel him. Take his hand and let him guide you to the right house."

We talked about Emma's Dad for a while. His wonderful attributes and how everyone loved him. I was able to describe his looks and nature to Emma which she took as confirmation. I asked Emma to put a big picture of her Dad in a frame and keep it in the kitchen as he LOVES being with you and the family!

The Lesson

Love knows no boundaries. The connection I felt between Evelyn and Emma and Andrew was so intense. In fact, I struggle to find the words to describe the feeling. People often ask me if I can contact their loved ones who have already passed over at will. I explain to them that I can't, they have to come to me. In fact, it is part of the deceased's lessons in life that if they want to come through, they need to learn how to do it themselves. It's not just an automatic thing to do. It's a conscious action made by the Soul.

I always tell people to expect the unexpected.

Hundreds of years ago people believed that if a spirit was to make contact, it was considered demonic and a priest would be called to perform a clearing. These days it's totally different.

Now more than ever before, people visit Psychics and Mediums to raise their own levels of Spiritual Awareness. We accept guidance from our Spirit Guides and Angels. We accept their love and guidance without question. We know it to be true. If they can come through to us, then we also know that we will be able to come through to our families when the time comes. I sense that there will be an increase in the work done by Psychics and Mediums in order to bring through all the people that now know they can.

Love is amazing. It was the love that Andrew had for Evelyn and Emma that brought him through for them in their readings. This is why it is incredibly important that we ensure we send our loved ones off with our love and with the comfort of knowing that they can come through to us should they want to.

Testimonial from Evelyn

Thank you very much for your reading today. It was amazing. You have helped me come to terms with my issues from the past. I feel much more relieved about my family situation and your suggestion to help them is much appreciated. I feel like a weight has been lifted.

Thank you for your compassion and insight. You have an amazing gift.

Lauren: Who You Gonna Call?

Dedicated to Lauren and Phil

I received a phone call from a distressed Phil one evening. Phil was very concerned about his wife and the goings on in their house. They both believed their house was haunted as lots of strange things were happening, mostly to Lauren.

We scheduled a time for me to come and visit. I asked Phil to ask Lauren to document everything that was happening to her and in the house with the date and time of the event so that I could review it when I came to visit, which I did a few evenings later.

As I stepped into the hallway after being greeted at the front door by a very agitated and stressed Lauren, she immediately asked me, "Do you feel anything in this house?" I said not. In fact, I had. But it was from Lauren, not anything suspicious.

Lauren and I looked at the list of events that had taken place over the previous week. She had heard someone walking around their house. She'd seen brown shadows, had felt pinned to the bed and had seen red and green orbs. Her dog would sit frozen in one spot, barking. She would constantly feel pin pricks on her legs. She'd seen a strange shape at the end of her bed. She'd felt the bed covers played with and a picture fell off the wall. Lauren was fighting tears. She looked so scared.

She asked me again, "Do you sense anyone here right now? Because I do. Do you know what's going on? I can't cope anymore. This is getting between my partner and I and we are trying for a baby but don't want to bring a baby into this environment."

Lauren and Phil had moved to their house two years before. Everything that was happening to Lauren now had happened to her in their previous house also. To me, it was simple.

"Lauren, you are psychic!" I just came out with it. "The Spirits are trying to get your attention. They need your help. This is your Soul's work. There is nothing to be scared of. Of course, you do not have to do this work if it frightens you. However, I sense that there are children involved here that you can help. They feel connected to you."

I continued, "Lauren, if a Spirit were to manifest itself in front of you and ask for help, you would probably die in shock. They cannot do that. So, Spirits try to get our attention in other ways. Which, it seems, they have been doing. Now that you know this, what are your thoughts about it? Would you like them to stop or would you like to help them?"

LAUREN: WHO YOU GONNA CALL?

Lauren didn't need time to think at all "I would love to help them, will you teach me how?"

We discussed steps she would need to take next and with her asking excellent questions, we covered a lot of ground that evening. We agreed to meet a few weeks later and I said that she could call me day or night if she felt she needed to.

With that, she walked me to the door. The Lauren that walked me to the door looked ten years younger. Calm, happy and focused. Completely different to the stressed out Lauren that opened the door to me a few hours earlier.

I have met with Lauren on a couple of occasions since. She has embraced her gift by using automatic writing. The power of Spirit never ceases to amaze me or teach me.

Kimberly: The Woman In The Mirror

Dedicated to Kimberly

Years ago when Kimberly looked in the mirror, she saw a gorgeous woman that exuded confidence and beauty. Today when Kimberly looks in the mirror she... Actually, Kimberly can't look herself in the mirror anymore, because she does not like what she sees.

When Kimberly came to me for a Reading, I was guided by my Team to act as a mirror and make her face her reality. This was one of the hardest Readings I've ever had to do and it certainly made me uncomfortable, getting angry at a stranger. I felt like I was caught between two worlds.

However, I am sure Kimberly got the message loud and clear and hopefully will never drink alcohol again. Kimberly needed to be confronted. And she was.

My rational mind and my Soul struggled with the path Spirit wanted me to take with Kimberly's Reading. I needed to be certain that what I was getting was accurate. Per-

KIMBERLY: THE WOMAN IN THE MIRROR

sonal judgement must stay out of a Reading.

Kimberly's Reading took place one evening not that long ago. I particularly like evening Readings as candles light the room providing a very welcoming atmosphere. My Team loved the energy in the room as well. However, when I led Kimberly into the room, everything changed. The energy changed. I felt anger, frustration, hostility, resentment and despair.

At the very beginning of our Reading, Kim told me all about how awful growing up had been for her. She told me how much she hated her parents. She told me that her dream in life was to have a table full of family for dinner, her playing the hostess to a tee. Her eyes filled with tears of longing.

I felt an energy take me over on behalf of Kimberly's teenage children. I also felt that Kimberly's kids were bringing themselves up. I felt that Kimberly's eldest child was in fact parenting his own mother. I sensed addiction. I was right.

I had no idea how this Reading was going to go. I'd never done a Reading like this before and I never want to do one like this again.

Kimberly talked about how men were attracted to her but explained that she didn't know which ones to have a relationship with. She also talked about how she drank herself to sleep every day. Kimberly drank in secret. Often disguising alcohol in water bottles.

While Kimberly spoke, my Team were encouraging me to talk to her about how much her kids miss her. That she's an absent mum. The whole family was merely existing. Going through the motions. She'd checked out of their lives long ago.

I told Kimberly that she needed to grow up and face her responsibilities rather than acting like a child when even her own kids didn't act the way she was. She didn't listen. So, Spirit raised the tone of my voice for impact. I found myself getting angrier and angrier. Spirits were coming through me telling Kimberly exactly what she needed to hear. It was tough.

As I listened to Kimberly justifying her drinking and smoking addictions, I suddenly realised that my Team had turned me into one of her children. She needed to see exactly what she was doing to them. But she wouldn't face it. So, I had to show her.

Kim was a single mother of four children. I began to sob. I told her how selfish she was, how self-centred she was. How could she call herself a mother, I asked. Spending her days and nights drinking. Spending her days working or sleeping. But spending none of her days or nights with her children.

I got the sense that one of her sons had taken the role of both father and mother in her family. Until then, Kim had in fact led a very blessed life. She was comfortable financially and wanted for nothing. She had four beautiful children. She held a job and had many friends. Life had been good to Kim.

It was Kim that had been hard on herself. She told me she was addicted to smoking and the high and the escape she got from alcohol. It made life so much easier to cope with. She hated her life. She simply couldn't see anything good about it.

Normally parents need to educate their children about the toxic effects alcohol can have on their lives. But Kimberly's kids already knew this. They saw the effects. They were the ones teaching their parent about the toxic effects it was already having on their family. But she wasn't listening. Coming from a stranger, who knew nothing about her, it seemed to sink in a little better.

By this time, Kim had started crying. She told me that she was merely existing. Nothing meant anything to her except the next man and getting drunk. She told me that she had even told her children she couldn't wait for them to move out and that they were an inconvenience to her.

I could feel my Team moving in for an intervention. I felt myself getting angrier and angrier minute by minute as Kimberly tried to justify her behaviour to me. I had taken on the role of her children and was speaking to her on behalf of her children.

I told her how much her kids missed her. How much they hated her behaviour and wished she could be like their friends' mothers. I told her about the vision I had of her in a hospital bed with her kids all around her after she had passed away. One of them said aloud, "Thank God she's gone. I just really hope there is no such thing as life after death as I don't want her to come through to me if I ever go to see a Psychic."

I said to Kim "If I told you you were only going to live

a couple more years, would that have an impact on you at all?" I described my vision to her and she started sobbing. So did I.

I was now pacing around the room begging her to be a mother to her children. My Team were working overtime for this Reading. I was so removed from my human self that I could do nothing else but trust them. They were determined to save this woman from self-destruction.

I sat back down at the table and reached out for Kimberly's hands. She held onto them tightly, tears streaming down her face.

"Kimberly," I said. "I am so sorry. You have come here to have a nice Reading this evening and it's been just awful. I'm not sure what you've come here to hear tonight but this is what Spirit wants you to see tonight."

Kimberly then said, "Marion, I have seen other Psychics and they always just seem to tell me what they think I want to hear and it all feels very general. You have given me tonight exactly what I do need to hear. Yes, I am shocked. But it's exactly what I need. Do I really only have that long to live?"

"Kimberly, I never ever tell people when their expiry date is due. But consider this. You have always told yourself that one day, you'll change. Well, you know what Kimberly? Today is that day. Today is one day. If you heed the warning given by my Team and your Guides today, you will live a long healthy life. But tonight, they needed to get your attention and the only way to do that was by telling you that you may not live much longer."

KIMBERLY: THE WOMAN IN THE MIRROR

"You need to be a Mum to your children. Those four children chose you for very good reasons. You are an amazingly loving person. I recommend that you reconnect with your kids. Sit down with all four of them. Have a round table discussion. Tell them that you love them and have finally seen the error in your ways and with their support you will from this day forward try harder than you ever have before to make it up to them. There's no need to over compensate. But there's every reason to love. I feel that right now you are simply existing. I recommend that one night a week you have a family night. The kids prepare dinner. No phones or internet and then after dinner you play a board game. Tell them you would like them to do it once a week. Spend time with each of them as individuals. Tell them what you love most about them. It's not a conversation, it's a statement. Kimberly, it's time to grow up. Be the kind of parent you wished that you had had yourself. Those kids chose you for a reason to be their Mum. Now be it."

I reminded Kimberly of what she told me about at the beginning of the Reading, about wishing she could have a family dinner with everyone and be the gleaming hostess. I told her that she had it already, with her own kids. Right there in front of her. Yet, she was choosing to neglect her kids and write herself off with alcohol to hide from how she really felt.

Kimberly and I sat quietly for a while, deep in our own thoughts. The anger had left me and love had returned to Kimberly's eyes. We were still holding hands across the table.

"Thank you," she whispered. "Thank you for not being like the others. You are like no other that I have ever seen. You have given me exactly what I needed tonight. You are truly gifted."

Tomorrow when Kimberly looks in the mirror, she will see a very strong, capable, wonderful person that was courageous enough to change. For the love of herself. For the love of her kids.

I never saw Kimberly again but she did refer one of her best friends to me who told me that Kimberly had told her that I was gifted and that Kimberly had in fact stopped drinking and was very active in her children's lives again. Things seemed to be going well for them all, particularly Kimberly. Because of seeing the change first hand, Kimberly's friend knew that it was right for her to come and see me also.

The Lesson

Honesty and authenticity are some of the biggest Spiritual lessons we have to learn in this life. When Kimberly came, I asked her to leave her human self in the other room to chat with my mine so that we could talk Soul to Soul.

Most of the time when people come to me for a Read-

KIMBERLY: THE WOMAN IN THE MIRROR

ing, I receive a feeling of immense love with the connections as they come through. I look forward to playing a very positive role in one's Spiritual journey.

Kimberly's Reading didn't feel like that at all. In fact, it was very draining, very emotional and very painful. It was my job to act as a mirror to Kimberly, reflecting her childrens' pain back to her.

Spirits (Guides) and spirits (alcohol) do not mix. The intervention and emotion experienced during this Reading is something I simply cannot put into words. It's really only something Kimberly and I share. But, if you come for a Reading, thinking that you can hide yourself from Spirit, think again. You are transparent.

A Spiritual Reading is exactly that. It's not about giving you the winning lotto numbers or your future husband or wife's name. It's about guiding you on your Spiritual journey through this life.

Be prepared to hear something you don't want to.

If you are given profound guidance for you in your life, are you prepared to listen?

Above: My son James and I after his contest win
Below: The glow on my wedding day

Above: Robert Bandy and I at the crash site in Yetna
Below: The official RAAF record of the crash

Above: Murni and I in Bali
Below: Murni and her daughter, Morny

Above: Murni's Warung in Ubud, Bali
Below: A young Murni

Lexi: Boyfriends and Kangaroos

Dedicated to Lexi

Lexi had been given a gift voucher to come and see me. She had never had a Reading before but was encouraged to go just so she could say she had experienced one. She had no expectations or questions and left everything up to me.

Once we had settled in with the obligatory serving of afternoon tea I provided Lexi with her first two names of significance: Beth and Damien. I told her that I felt that Beth really needed her at the moment and was glad to have her support. Through tears Lexi told me that Beth was a very dear friend of hers who was suffering with cancer. I suggested that she hold a little birthday party for Beth as I felt it would mean the world to her. Birthday cake, streamers, balloons and whistles would really pick up Beth's spirits.

If Lexi was shocked by my knowledge of Beth, she

was left utterly speechless by my knowledge of Damien. "Damien, was my first ever boyfriend," she said. "Whilst he was a really nice guy he caused some unrest in my family, especially with Mum, and the rift remains in place today."

Lexi began to cry and I was moved to sit next to her and hold her close. My Team gave me the words to say next. "Lexi, you are a beautiful Soul. If only there were more like you, the world would be a much happier place. You are a teacher for your Mum. You have the best spiritual values that a person can. I speak of tolerance, compassion, sincerity, kindness, empathy, love and forgiveness. These are the very values your Mum needs to learn. Whilst you feel she doesn't accept you for the person she thinks you are, that's not your fault. She doesn't accept most people, her expectations are too high. Your Mum doesn't really know you and hasn't tried to get to know you. You are perfect just the way you are. Don't change for anyone. You are one of the most together people I have ever met. You in fact, inspire me!"

Lexi and I enjoyed the feeling that came through during her Reading, and we sat awhile alone with our thoughts. Suddenly, I started laughing and moved back to my own seat.

"Why are you laughing?" Lexi asked me.

"Well, for some reason I am seeing a boxing kangaroo. His name is Kevin. I really don't know why. I must have a vivid imagination!"

"No, it's not your imagination," she said, "Kevin's our pet kangaroo. We haven't seen him for weeks actually. Is he ok?"

"Yep, got himself a girlfriend it seems."

We both laughed which did us both the world of good after the intensity of Lexi's Reading. Readings always come to a natural conclusion and as Lexi stood up to leave, she asked to hug me. I will remember her hug forever because her heart hugged mine and I knew I had set her free to begin her own spiritual journey.

Sharon: The L Word

Dedicated to Sharon

Sharon was referred to me by a dear friend of hers that had experienced my Reading style first hand and knew it would be right for Sharon. It was a glorious summer afternoon when Sharon came to see me and we decided to sit outside on the deck in a relaxed atmosphere.

Sharon came to ask me about the L word; love. As I normally do at the beginning of each Reading, I gave Sharon the names of all the people that had come through for her. The three most important were: Bill, Winne and Fred.

These three names felt very significant. Upon hearing them, Sharon was immediately moved to tears.

"Bill was my Grandfather and Winnie and Fred are one person – My Grandma – Winifred!"

I suddenly felt a sharp pain that I thought related to the unhealthy lunch I'd recently consumed. I flinched, which made Sharon jump.

"Ooh, that hurt," I said.

Sharon responded by saying, "My Grandpa Bill was fixing a fence when he got shot through it and died. To this day we do not know why or by whom. There was a real controversy around the incident after he died. Are you able to find out why? Or by whom perhaps?"

I checked with my Team but was unable to throw any light on the situation at all. I was shocked at the intensity of the Reading. There was no further information at all relating to the incident and I refuse to make anything up just to make the story sound better. I am given what I am given and that's what I pass on. I am just the Psychic Postie. We spent the rest of the time discussing all the other people associated with the names that came through for Sharon that day.

One thing about living in Australia in summer is that you know exactly when the sun is about to set because the mosquitoes come out in force. Sharon and I had spent a lovely couple of hours like old friends sitting on the deck chatting about love and life itself. With the interruption from the mosquitoes we were quickly brought back into the real world and realised that we'd been talking for ages and both needed to get on with our real life responsibilities.

Sharon came to me as a stranger, but left as a friend.

The Lesson

Whilst the main message in Sharon's Reading was about the two significant contacts that came through for

SHARON: THE L WORD

her, Sharon really came to ask me about love. A lot of people I see come to me for reassurance that they will find love in their life again. Love is something we all experience in our lives at one point or other. As someone close to me once said after my break up, "We all experience love once in our life time. If we find it a second time we are really lucky."

This was the main reason Sharon came to me and sure, there was information about love for her. I haven't shared it all here because of course, it was very personal.

Love makes us feel good. Love makes us feel wanted. Love brings out the best in us. It makes us want to share, laugh and set goals. It gives our lives a sense of purpose and direction.

Love also tears us apart when we lose it. We are in love with love, and well we should be.

Leslie: A Friend Taken Too Soon

Dedicated to Leslie and Wendy

Leslie bounded into my lounge room larger than life.

"How can I help you Leslie?" I asked, trying to ground her.

"I've got so much going on Marion, I just don't know where to turn. My whole life feels like everything's up in the air and nothing's going right for me. My health, my weight, my love life, my racing heartbeat. And there's menopause, my lack of motivation and study. Not to mention my job and the troublemakers I work with. Why can't I make friends? I never feel good enough. I just can't seem to prioritise my life or my purpose or direction. I really hope you can help me. I felt compelled to come and talk to you today. I can't tell you why other than that I was directed to. So here I am. Fix me."

I might be Psychic, but a magic wand I don't have.

WOW! Ok! Normally before my Guest arrives for their Reading with me, I chat with my Team letting them know who is coming. I ask for any visitors for my guest to come through with their names and messages. I ensure my Gatekeeper is in place to protect all parties. I generally get names for people before they've even arrived for their Reading. Leslie's was no different.

Wendy came through to me a few hours before Leslie arrived. Once Leslie and I had worked through her reasons for coming to see me we took a short comfort break and made a fresh pot of tea.

"Leslie, I'd like to ask you about Wendy. Wendy came through to me this morning before you arrived and asked me to ask you to 'Never forget me. I feel that you have. I haven't forgotten about you. Please put the photo of me into a frame and put me in your kitchen where I can see everything that's going on and you can never forget about me.'"

As often happens when people receive profound messages like this, Leslie's tough exterior crumbled. I went on, "Wendy knows the real you! She wants you to know that the real you is worth knowing. She loved and still loves the real you! You've just hidden her away. Bring her back out to dance to the music on the radio."

"Leslie," I said next, "You've been telling yourself that one day you will take control of your life back. Today is one day. You have all the information and confirmation you need within you, all I needed to do was remind you about it."

"You know what," Leslie said, "You're right. I have known everything you've told me about today. I just haven't listened. Thank you so much. I feel so very much lighter and happier now."

And with that, she was gone. But not without a hug and a wink over her shoulder as she walked to her car. She did tell me why Wendy was significant, but that's between Leslie and Wendy.

The Lesson

Ah, the power of Spirit when it hits home. I just love watching the effect it has on people. We all have a higher self, so why do we choose to ignore it? The Soul knows so much more than the mind does. We all ask or pray for help, and then more often than not turn away from the advice if we don't hear exactly what we wanted to. I too, am guilty.

Trust yourself. Listen to your conscience, intuition or whatever you want to call it. Because those messages come from your higher self. This is how your guides communicate with you.

Of course, if you ask for the help, you need to listen to the answers.

Uncle George and his Girls

Dedicated to Uncle George

One day, I met with a unique group of women on a houseboat in Tailem Bend. After introducing myself to them, fielding their questions and reassuring the first timers, I was escorted to a lovely lounge room at the back of the boat where I settled myself in for the day.

Rather than go into detail about each Reading, I would like to focus on a thread that ran through all of their Readings. I knew nothing about these women and didn't even know they were all related until after they were all done.

Danni

Danni was my first Reading. As soon as she sat down I told her that George was here with her today for her birthday. She was in tears within seconds. "Oh, how wonderful, that's my Uncle!" she exclaimed, "We were very close." Danni's Uncle George gave her some good advice regarding her personal situation, which I believed she would take on board.

Sally

As soon as Sally sat down, I immediately had George back with me. This time he brought guests, Aunty Fiona and Elly. Sally confirmed that George was her Uncle. Somehow, I still hadn't connected the dots. Uncle George asked me to teach Sally about tolerance and forgiveness as he felt that they were two lessons that she needed to learn in order to help her personal situation.

"Listen to your heart dear girl," George told her.

Jaqui

Jaqui brought with her the most beautiful energy. In fact, they all did. This was certainly a very special group of women.

I was able to connect with Jaqui straight away through the names Cyril, William and, of course, George. I saw she was going on a cruise holiday. I also asked Jaqui if she was looking at moving off the boat and onto a property - a large property with old established homes.

She said, "Yes, should I move there?" I told her that I thought it was a really good idea and that I could see it very clearly. I also saw that more people would be living there.

Emily

When Emily came in for her Reading, I felt a real heaviness around her. I felt like she was carrying the weight of the world on her shoulders. As the names started to come through for her, I could see why she was so burdened.

Anthony was the first name that came through for Emily and he had a special message for her, "Tell Emily that I'm sorry. I messed up big time." With that, he was gone. Emily told me that Anthony hung himself 13 years prior.

Frank came through soon after. He told me to remind Emily about the something special that happened at a funeral he was at whilst he was still alive. Emily knew exactly what he was referring to. Turns out Frank had also committed suicide.

Poor Emily, all this sadness around her. But again, Uncle George was there to comfort her. Sadly, he was unable to help her with the most important question of all, "Who is my Father?"

Charmaine

Charmaine was the only one that George didn't come through to. I did give Charmaine the names of Alfred and Joseph. Turns out Joe was Alfred's second name. Charmaine was thankful for the connection.

CAUGHT BETWEEN TWO WORLDS

Geraldine

Geraldine felt that lately life was like Groundhog Day. She was becoming disillusioned with her life. I knew that Geraldine worked in an office but I didn't feel like she was an office kind of person. She confirmed that she was a Ranger and was based in an office. She revealed to me that all the women present that day were part of the local Ngarrindjeri group of Indigenous Australians.

Geraldine had 3 main visitors. There was Phillip, her cousin, who apologised about the car seat incident. This made her chuckle. Then there was Albert who was a friend and used to send her on tourism conferences. Then, you guessed it, George was back. He described himself as her main man. Geraldine laughed and agreed.

Natalie

As soon as Natalie sat down, I asked her who in her family drove a blue car? She confirmed that her son did. I told her that if nothing else, the thing she needs to take away from today's Reading was to ask her son to slow down and not use the phone whilst driving.

Three profound names came through as a connection for Natalie. Matthew, Tim and obviously, George. It was then that I got the sense that George was related to all of these women in some way. I felt like he had been their go-to guy.

Later, the women confirmed that he was related to all

of them and was certainly their mentor and guide in life. He was held in great esteem by their Indigenous Group. It seemed he would also be their Guide in after-life.

I had written out the notes for each woman and asked them not to discuss them with the others until I came out at the end of the day so we could discuss as a group.

I would like to honour all the women at the Reading in Tailem Bend on that Sunday, along with all the members of their Ngarrindjeri Group. This was one day I would never forget.

The Lesson

We are all Souls. We are all connected through our Souls, regardless of nationality, culture, race or religion. If Spirit has a message for you, it will be delivered.

In this case, over and over and over and over again by their beloved and highly esteemed Uncle George.

Testimonial from Sally

I'm a very sceptical person by nature and have put off having a reading for years. I spent 30 minutes with Marion today and I feel as if I have no weight left on my shoulders. Thank you so much Marion, I can't express in words how grateful I am for the gift you have given me. I will be booking another appointment soon.

Testimonial from Emily

I was amazed at what I got in my Reading today. I did not expect what I received but was pleased, relieved and thankful. Marion, you are 100% genuine and your Gift is amazing. I hope to see you again.

Chloe: Children as Teachers

Dedicated to Chloe and her two beautiful children

Sometimes Readings take you right into the heart of a family's pain, showing you the worst of society. It's never easy, but its part and parcel of what I do. I remember I once received a desperate call for help from a beautiful woman who had never had a Reading before. Her name was Chloe and she respected and believed in the work that Readers do, even though she didn't really understand it.

Chloe was a single Mum of a beautiful boy and girl, both of whom, it took me no time to learn, were Old Souls. They were gifted with the Gift of Knowing. Both were in Chloe's life as teachers for her own spiritual journey.

Let me describe Chloe. She arrived for her Reading just as my parents were leaving. Chloe actually offered my Mum a hug which touched my Mum's heart. There were tears before we'd even started. I sensed Chloe's apprehension and desperation and I quietly prayed to my Team to help her. Chloe had brought a serious issue with her that was somewhat beyond my experience and I trusted that the words she needed that day would come through. Indeed they did.

After a general chit chat about the weather and Chloe's children, I asked her to tell me about the pain she was in and what brought her to see me that day. All I could see was pure torment in the eyes of this beautiful, warm, caring, compassionate woman.

"I only have one question," she said haltingly, "You see I am involved in a bitter custody battle after separating from my ex, who was violent towards me and the children." Her eyes had filled with tears and I prayed silently to my Team. "Please, please tell me that my two year old Son will come home alive after this week's visit," Chloe pleaded.

I reached out and held her hand. "Yes, yes he will," I was able to immediately reassure her that her two year old son would indeed be returned to her alive after that week's custody visit.

"My daughter, aged four, refuses to go to see her father and sometimes says things that really worry me. My son has come home from custody visits miserable and sometimes with bruises. I photograph everything and document everything as we are going through Court to try and get settlement and closure on our separation. He is doing everything in his power to get the kids taken away from me when in fact it's him they don't want to be with. He is manipulating and poisoning them against me and my parents. If it weren't for the help I get from my parents, I just don't think I would be able to cope. I can't take anymore.

CHLOE: CHILDREN AS TEACHERS

Please tell me what you think will happen to my family, Marion."

Chloe and I discussed her very real fears, together with my Team, for a long time that afternoon. We discussed the benefits of talking to her Guides and Angels. We also talked about the two Angels that are her children and how very blessed she is to have them in her life. I sensed too that her daughter was very intuitive. That even though she was only 4 years old, she had a most beautiful sense of universal wisdom that could give Chloe comfort and strength during these hard months. Chloe told me that she would love for me to meet with her daughter again to help her with these gifts.

The emotional intensity of Chloe's Reading was none like I had ever experienced before. The responsibility of counselling Chloe through her messages felt extra special that day. I felt caught between two worlds because I didn't feel at all worldly qualified to help Chloe, but knew that I could trust my Team to guide me. This is where faith comes in.

Chloe was in a very fragile state of mind. There was one thing I knew for sure though. That that weekend at least, her son would come home alive. I could reassure her that much.

By the end of the Reading, Chloe expressed her great relief and comfort for our chat and left shortly afterwards looking at least ten years younger than when she walked in two hours earlier.

I have seen Chloe and her children since. To say that

she inspires me would be an understatement. She always had the strength inside of her, she'd just misplaced it awhile. It was my job to reintroduce her to herself and her mission in life. In my mind, heart and Soul, I know this Mum will win.

Testimonial from Chloe– (Chloe describes her heartache regarding domestic violence)

Meeting Marion at the exact moment in which I did I can only describe as one of the miracles of the universe. Over time I have become a true believer of life giving you opportunities in the moment in which they'll be most beneficial, when we are able to deal with them. Sometimes you must reach rock bottom in order for you to be forced into putting yourself back onto your right path in life.

For me, I found one of these moments when I chose to leave my husband and the other just before reaching out to Marion.

Being a mother of two young children living with domestic violence, there comes a point when there is no option but to leave. Even after leaving, worry and fear were still a constant part of my everyday life to the point that at times it was crippling. I found myself going through the court system trying desperately to keep my children safe. Despite my best efforts our system is set up for both parents to have the right to have a relationship with their children, regardless of the parent's prior history.

I left my whole life behind to give my children a fu-

CHLOE: CHILDREN AS TEACHERS

ture that was free from abuse by their father. I then found myself being told that I have to encourage my children to spend unsupervised time with him, the person I most feared.

My eldest daughter still refuses to see her father, but my youngest son is being forced to simply because the courts see him as too young to decide for himself.

Worry and stress was taking me over as my whole focus was on trying to protect my children in a situation where I had no control. I could not escape the constant court appointments at which the father continued to demand more contact time and freedom.

On top of worrying about my children's safety and raising two young children, I also was trying desperately to understand and help my children deal with their own roller-coaster of emotions and at times violent behaviour.

My family have been a constant pillar of strength throughout everything but, of course, they too were all feeling the same stress and worry regarding the safety of my children.

Fear for my children was the sole reason I reached out to Marion. It was on this day that our lives truly changed and that crippling fear was replaced with hope and a calmness and inner strength that is difficult to describe.

Marion gave me the permission to now stop worrying and rather focus on enjoying spending time with my two very precious children. She was able to reassure me that both my children will be safe. That in itself brought tears to my eyes and a feeling of such relief to my heart. Marion was able to tell me that my son will not be seriously hurt in any life threatening manner.

Lastly, Marion was able to reassure me that my ex will walk away. At that moment I felt that he lost all the power he once had over me. I have gone from being fearful and powerless to realising that he is an insignificant person in our lives and one day in the near future he will be nothing but a distant memory. My two children will not only be safe but will live happy and fulfilled lives. Marion gave me new hope and the motivation to keep strong for my family.

Marion was able to share the most incredible gift insight into who my children truly are. Knowing this has empowered me to better understand and work with them in a way that encourages their inner strength and builds their self-confidence. I am now on the path of enjoying and embracing my children's unique gifts.

Since working with Marion the dark clouds that were hovering over have lifted and I feel tremendously blessed and honoured that two remarkable young children chose me to be their parent. I am now able to focus on the positive things in life and truly understand what it means for our soul to be happy.

I may be the parent, but Marion's wise words and insight have shown me that my Children are in fact also my teachers. Some of the most important lessons I've ever learned have come from them. They have taught me to live in the moment and that love is everything. Life may at times be spiralling around us but our inner peace always comes from within. We need to slow down life in order for

CHLOE: CHILDREN AS TEACHERS

us to enjoy the moments that truly matters.

My daughter said this to me the other day, "I think the most important thing in life is love. Cos if you don't love anyone you don't have any friends. That's why love is so special. I love you Mummy."

Marion has shown me strength I never knew I had. She's gifted me the peace of mind that my heart desperately needed by reminding me to have fun with my children. She's brought laughter back into our home. I will be forever grateful for the help, support and constant friendship from Marion. She is a truly gifted and beautiful person. Fear no longer has a hold on me!

Sheridan: Elders in the Garden

Dedicated to Sheridan and Trinity.

Sheridan's Mum, Maggie, rang me one day seeking help for her daughter, Sheridan. Maggie never told me what was going on but told me she would like to make an appointment for them both to come and see me. I booked them both in for a Reading in early January 2016. I was told by my Team that I would really like Sheri.

Once we were settled with our coffee and chocolates, I was able to connect with Sheri immediately by giving her the names Simon, Trinity and Ben. Ben was the father of Sheri's son and Simon worked with Sheri's boyfriend, Adam. Simon was Trinity's Dad. Trinity had tragically passed away as a tiny baby. Simon and Adam worked at a local spa retreat. There were plans in progress for a memorial to be built in the gardens for Trinity. Sheri explained that whilst she wanted to attend the service, the reason she had come to see me was to work out exactly why she couldn't walk in the grounds of that retreat. She really wanted to attend the upcoming memorial service but just could not bring herself to go inside the grounds.

Sheri said that she'd recently been having dreams about the retreat. She saw gates at the front but was unable to walk through them. The memorial was being planned for a particular location in the gardens. She said that her dream showed her that the site was a sacred Indigenous site. Her dream had told her that three sisters had been murdered on that land before it was developed by white man and that the Indigenous Elders had yet to be acknowledged.

Sheri paused a moment after recounting all of this and then gave me the most outstanding piece of information yet. She said that recently, Adam came home and told her that three Indigenous Elders had walked all the way from Queensland and taken up position at the very spot the memorial was planned for. No one knows who they are and no one knew they were coming. No one told them anything about what was planned for the Retreat. They simply turned up and gave no indication that they were planning to leave.

There was no apparent connection between the retreat and the three Elders. Sheri believed that the Indigenous Elders knew about the murder of the three sisters and that's why they'd come. If that was the case, then what Sheri had was not a dream, but a vision.

Suddenly, everything became surreal. I felt like I'd been taken out of my body. I remember the feeling well. With a start, I turned to face Sheri and told her that I had just been shown that she was one of the sisters that had been murdered and that's why she was finding it so hard to go inside the gates. I then saw an image of an Indigenous man with grey hair. He was holding his hand out to her and said that he would walk through the gates with her.

He told me that the gates were symbolic only and represented the border between Sheri being white and Indigenous. The gates were just to show her that she could cross back at any time. This Elder told me that he would be there that day at 4pm and would hold his hand out to her and that she should take it. He said the only word he would say was sorry.

I then saw an image of the two of them standing side by side at the memorial site holding hands. The images faded and I was back in the room with Sheri who was smiling broadly.

"It all makes sense," she said, "I'm one of those sisters. It all makes sense. I better leave now if I am to be there at 4pm. How can I ever thank you?" she asked.

I suggested Sheri undertake historical research on the area as it will reveal many secrets. I also encouraged her to apply for work with the Indigenous Commission, preferably as a Youth Counsellor. She advised that that was exactly what she was thinking of doing.

Sheri told me that she felt enormous comfort from our Reading and that she would go straight to the Retreat after our Reading. I sensed her life was about to start.

SHERIDAN: ELDERS IN THE GARDEN

Testimonial from Sheridan

Marion, thank you from my heart and soul for giving me your time, love and energy. Clarification about the Indigenous Australians was just what I needed and I will embrace all your insights with love, excitement and Joy.

You're significant and amazing with a huge heart.

Testimonial from Maggie

Many beliefs and truths I have found with you. I can't thank you enough for my own future guidance, with joy I can now step into a new day. As a Mother to Sheri, I'm overjoyed for the love, guidance, compassion and understanding of the Spiritual world you have been able to share.

Many blessings to you Marion. I'm sure we'll meet again.

Diane: Seeking Justice

Dedicated to Diane

As I always tell people, we keep on learning until all our fingers are the same length. Diane came to me as a Teacher. She didn't realise it and neither did I, until I'd left her home. She greeted me at her front door, manoeuvring a walking frame.

"Come on in, don't mind this silly thing, it gets in the way of everything," she laughed gleefully. I liked her already.

After giving me a personal guided tour of all her beautiful birds in their cages, we settled down for her Reading. I think really she just wanted to chat about Spirituality, which I'm always happy to do. She was very insightful and I told her so.

Diane has four beautiful children; three boys and a girl. She's an awesome mother. Her children and husband come first, always. Housework last.

Many years ago, when Diane was with her first hus-

DIANE: SEEKING JUSTICE

band and her baby boy was 9 months old, she was struck down by a virus and felt very unwell for a long time. One day she collapsed on the floor and her ex-husband called an ambulance. She was given a choice of preferred hospitals and consequently still regrets the choice she made that day.

In her younger years Diane had made some very poor choices in regard to drug taking, so what happened that day turned out to be somewhat ironic. She ended up in the corridor of a major hospital, slipping in and out of consciousness. She heard nurses passing by, commenting that she was on drugs. They'd say she just needed to sleep it off. As a result, 18 hours went by and Diane became severely dehydrated. She fell into unconsciousness and her kidneys shut down. Long story short, because of the inattention in that hospital, she was left with brain damage and has required a walker to support herself ever since.

Life would never be the same again for Diane. During the time that she was home recuperating, her nine month old son died. He had broken ribs and a fractured skull. She believes firmly that her ex-husband lost his temper and caused the injuries from which he died. He was never charged, but Diane knows in her heart that this is the case.

Diane came to me with just one question in her heart, would her son ever receive justice? As this was an extremely personal question, I respect her request that the dialogue not be included in this story.

Diane is surrounded by an incredible group of angels, giving her the strength every day to put one foot in front of the other, literally. I saw one of the angels standing at the foot of Diane's bed. I described this young Angel to Diane as a fair haired toddler holding a basket. He was saying, "Mummy you can put your worries in the basket, I am closer to heaven and can help you." Boy, that was a tough one to see.

Whilst some people might feel sorry for Diane, I don't. If I had known her before her illness, then I might have. Back then, she made bad decisions in regards to health and substance abuse. These days, however, I see a courageous woman. We could all learn a lot from her.

She says it as it is. She doesn't play mind games and puts herself first, then her family. This is the way she copes. If she neglected her own needs she would be no good to her family. She's is a wonderful listener and always ready to impart the wisdom learnt through her traumatic experiences. Diane lives in her Soul State 95% of the time.

I felt like Diane was the Angel that I needed.

The Lesson

It is my absolute privilege to be able to meet and Read for so many people. I never time my Readings. I tell people they take as long as they need to. Sometimes that's up to two and a half hours, sometimes as short as 30 minutes. I always allow time for people to ask questions of a spiritual nature and to talk about their own experiences of a paranormal nature or about their own journey. I am constantly surprised at the power of the Spirit and the way magic is weaved into our everyday lives.

Many people are forced onto their Spiritual Journey by way of a personal crisis. Sometimes these crises are caused by factors out of our control and sometimes they are caused by us. Regardless, how many times have you heard people say that even though something really traumatic and bad happened to them, their life is much better because of it.

Murni: An Empty Seat at the Bar

Dedicated to Murni and Morny

I first became interested in Murni's life history about six years ago while researching a unique place to stay in Ubud, Bali. I was looking for a forest experience. Murni was the first woman to ever set up a Warung (roadside restaurant) in Ubud.

Her restaurant remains in place today, small and very friendly. The food, staff, ambience and décor is inviting. In fact, the whole establishment feels very comfortable. When you know her, you see it's very Murni. The little gift store alongside is the perfect place to purchase quality gifts and souvenirs.

I used to visit Bali often. On occasions, I would help out in local orphanages and practice my Bhasa, an Indonesian language. I had a lot of fun with the children in the orphanages. They would teach me so much about life itself. From them I learned that the simpler the life, the better. Even in orphanages in Bali, families still come first.

MURNI: AN EMPTY SEAT AT THE BAR

The children come first. Each time I came home from Bali, I would declutter and simplify my life in order to enjoy it more. You've heard the saying 'less is more'? Well, it certainly is. The Balinese are an inspiring, humble, loving race.

I always loved the feel of Ubud. Over the last 10 to 15 years the tourism traffic has exploded and the whole place has become more westernised. That's why Murni and her story appealed to me. She was the original and much respected Matriarch in Ubud.

Generally, she allowed for people to visit with her at her home. Sadly, each time I was there, she was travelling overseas.

In 2014, my friend Nairina and I rented accommodation 20 kilometres out of Ubud that used to belong to Murni. It was called Murni's 3, one of her original homes. It is now rented out as short term accommodation and comes complete with staff to cater for your every need. Our most significant need (I use the term need loosely here) was to have our breakfast next to the infinity pool, overlooking the forest and listening to the roosters crowing on humid but fresh mornings.

Life was good in Murni's world. On each occasion that I travelled to Ubud I would enquire as to whether Murni was available to see visitors. One day, I was told that she was very unwell and they weren't sure how long she was going to live. As distressing as that was, I just knew that one day I would get to meet her. I also knew it would be special.

In March 2015, my now ex-husband asked me for a divorce. I was devastated. But that's a whole other book! My best friend Jennifer suggested we go to Bali together with our other best friend, Nairina. She suggested we stay in her Time Share accommodation in Nusa Dua. I said, "No need to ask me twice, just tell me when and where and I'll be there with sarongs on!"

It was exactly what I needed. Naturally, Ubud was on my itinerary. It's is the best place in Bali to buy silver jewellery. And buy jewellery we did. Almost all day long. The girls knew that I wanted to have dinner at Murni's Restaurant that night. I was hoping to be able to see Murni on that trip and asked the waitress if she was around. After phoning her residence, she came back to our table and told me that Murni was unavailable that evening due to personal appointments. Again, I was disappointed.

Nonetheless, we enjoyed our first cocktail sitting next to the open windows overlooking the river. The food, as usual, was delicious. As we bantered with the waitress, I felt a presence and looked up the stairs towards the doorway that led out to the road. What? Wait! Murni was standing in the doorway looking at me. Was she really there? I wasn't sure. My girlfriends saw the change in my demeanour and followed my gaze.

Murni was in fact standing there, looking straight at me! Our eyes locked and she started walking down the stairs straight towards me without breaking eye contact. I stood up and she held out her hand saying, "Welcome to my Restaurant, I feel that I am meant to meet you." We held hands like old friends.

MURNI: AN EMPTY SEAT AT THE BAR

I was stunned. Murni continued, "I never come into my Restaurant these days. I have very capable staff and prefer to keep to myself. But tonight, I felt compelled to come. I can't explain it. You are obviously the reason."

I introduced myself and my girlfriends to her. Murni and I were still holding hands so I said, "Murni, I have been trying to meet you for years. I have been following your life story. I have your book and I admire and respect all that you have achieved in your life. I am so glad to finally meet you in person!"

She replied, "I was meant to meet you tonight. I have never experienced a connection like this with anyone before. You are obviously here for a reason. Let me introduce my daughter Morny to you."

Morny was exactly like her Mother: beautiful, radiant, gracious, humble and wise. Murni asked if she could join us at the table for awhile, "We don't have to be anywhere do we Morny?"

Morny seemed reluctant to intrude on our dinner and reminded her Mother that they had had a busy and long day attending a friend's wedding. She also reminded her that her children were being babysat and really, the sitter should go home to her own family. But she could see that the request in her Mother's eyes was genuine and she agreed that they would stay for a few minutes.

The waitress brought over two extra chairs. Murni and Morny did indeed stay a while longer. Four hours longer, in fact. As we ate dinner, I invited Murni to tell about herself and her life. Her life had been both tragic and interesting; filled with love, disappointment, loss and emotion. By the time she'd finished, our dinners were almost untouched. She was captivating.

The atmosphere suddenly became electric. A male, a Spirit, had joined us at the table. Whilst Nairina, Morny and Murni were deep in conversation, I reached out to Jennifer and motioned to her that I was listening to Spirit, asked if she had a pen and paper I could use. Jennifer immediately knew what was going on.

I had zoned out of the dinner and listened to my visitor. Here's what he said, "My name is Peter Randall." As I wrote down his surname, he corrected me as I had spelt it wrong. "Murni was like a Mum to me. She wasn't around when I passed over a short while ago and I was never able to tell her what she meant to me. Please would you let her know how grateful I am for all the advice she ever gave me and for always listening and never judging me. I used to sit at the bar on the bar stool in the corner on the second floor. As far as I know my bar stool is still there. Ask her about it, please? Also, Murni is not well. Please ask Morny to tell her Mum how much she loves her, and vice versa. Ask Morny to tell her Mum what it is that she loves most about her before it's too late."

I had tears rolling down my cheeks. I felt all eyes on me. Here we go again. It was now clear to me why I was here. I was to reunite Murni and Peter. Jennifer and Nairina knew immediately what was going on. I held the napkin with Peter's name on it in my hand.

Murni and Morny looked completely bewildered and

MURNI: AN EMPTY SEAT AT THE BAR

couldn't work out what was going on. I had to explain, "Murni, Morny… I have something to tell you but I'm not sure how to start. I think I've just worked out why you were meant to come here to the Restaurant tonight to meet me. You see, I have the Gift of being a Psychic and sometimes a Medium. Tonight is one of those times. I have a man here with me in Spirit who told me that he passed only recently and he never got to say thank you or goodbye to you, Murni. He gave me his name as Peter Randall which I understood to be Randell, but he kept correcting me. He told me he used to sit at the bar on the second floor."

"Oh yes, yes. I know him. Yes, he was such a wonderful person. He used to sit at the bar stool downstairs in the corner," said Murni. Oddly, I had actually taken note of that particular bar stool when I went to the bathroom on the same floor. It stood out to me, now I knew why. Murni continued, "He passed away a few months ago whilst I was overseas. I can't believe this! This is wonderful and so very special. No wonder I am here tonight. Do you know what? Apparently, no one has sat in his stool since he passed."

"Murni, I have more messages, for both of you."

"Peter told me that you are not well. He has asked me to ask the both of you to tell each other how much you love each other. When is the last time you did that?"

This time it was Morny's turn to respond.

"I don't think I ever have, have I Ma? We don't really do that," she said.

Murni replied, "No, we haven't but I'd really like to. I know it's an important thing to do."

I continued, "Morny, Peter asks that you tell your Mum what it is that you love most about her. And what the most important lesson she's taught you is."

I looked around the table. There was not a dry eye. I held onto Jennifer's hand tightly. She was sitting on my right. I held onto Murni's hand tightly. She was sitting on my left.

"I'm so sorry," I said, "Sometimes when these things happen, they just take over. Please accept my apologies but I believe that the message is very important for all of you, even Peter."

"It's ok. I believe that there is a lot more to life than we know about. I am a very Spiritual person and I believe every word that you are saying. You could not have known about Peter sitting on the bar stool downstairs or how close we were or that I wasn't in Ubud when he passed. I trust you and I trust that Spirit brought us together tonight. As I said earlier, I rarely come to the Restaurant these days."

I looked at both Murni and Morny. The love between Mother and Daughter was indeed tangible. They were identical in looks, personality and Spirit. Murni would always live on in Morny.

By now it was dark outside. The sound of the crickets in the creek below together with the warm glow from the flickering candlelight allowed us to enjoy the specialness of those moments.

"Morny, please find a special time in private to say these things to your Mum. I know and can feel by looking into your eyes that it's important," I said.

"I would like to say it right here and right now," Mum said to her daughter.

"Oh, it's ok, you can do it in private," I interjected.

"No Marion," Murni said as she took my hand again, "This is something we have never done for each other and if it hadn't been for you bringing our messages through tonight, it would never have been said before I died. I would like to do it right here, right now and I would be honoured to do this in front of you and your special friends. Now is the perfect time."

"Yes, I agree," said Morny.

Nairina, Jennifer and I exchanged a teary glance. Poor Jennifer was trying to take it all in whilst videoing and taking photos for my benefit as I knew I would not remember all the facts once I came back into my body. The three of us exchanged a knowing smile that our hearts knew to interpret as love and the power of Spirit. In that moment, they too had become caught between two worlds.

Then Mother and Daughter turned to look at each other and said their peace. And I mean their peace. Not their piece. To say the moment was special would be an absolute understatement. To witness their love and dedication was spirituality in its rawest form.

Jen, Nairina and I looked at each other with tears streaming down our cheeks and whispered "I love you" to each other. These weren't token words said to make someone feel good. They were words deep from within our hearts and Souls.

Life for all of us would never be the same again.

The Lesson

Sometimes, with my permission, Spirit just takes over my energy and changes it. I've been told that people are attracted to me like a magnet without knowing why. When I go out, it seems that Spirit always arranges for me to meet someone who really needs a message from me that makes a difference in their lives at that exact moment in time.

I cannot explain it. Many people have tried to explain it to me. I feel the change within me. If you can remember what it's like to be in love; you know, that giddy, high, butterflies in the tummy feeling? Well that's what it's like for me. This is how I recognise when something special is going to happen.

This is exactly what happened at Murni's Warung on that hot April night in 2015. I know to trust. Spirit takes care of the rest.

John: Fright Night

Dedicated to John

John had been to see me on a couple of occasions. I found him to be someone very in tune with his higher self. I was always very interested to hear about his experiences after meditation. He was incredibly insightful and wise. I enjoyed listening to him.

At one stage, John had trouble sleeping. He said that sometimes he would dream about very ugly spirits with red teeth. He would then wake up frozen and unable to move. I really wasn't sure what was going on, so I asked him to monitor the situation.

One afternoon I received a distress call from him, "Marion, I can't take it anymore. The dreams have been getting worse. I no longer feel like they're dreams. They feel real now. The entities are real. Last night was the worst. I ended up getting up and getting one of my crystals and waved it around the air telling them to leave me alone and to go to the light. I did this for hours but they wouldn't go away.

CAUGHT BETWEEN TWO WORLDS

The bedroom was freezing and I could see my breath. I felt scared and out of my depth. I just didn't know what to do so I went to sleep in the spare bedroom and locked the door behind me. I eventually fell into a disturbed sleep and when I awoke in the morning, I immediately thought of you and knew that I had to ring you and ask for your help."

Accustomed as I am now to feeling my Team take over my Higher Self, it's not always easy. I told John I would be there about 8pm that night. He sounded ever so grateful.

At 8:30pm that evening, John and I were sitting at his dining table talking about the events when suddenly I saw the entities John had been describing. Oh my goodness, they were hideous! But really, they were just humans wearing masks. After all, there is no such thing as evil Spirits. That might sound like an odd thing for a Psychic to say, but I know it to be true. These masks that they wear show us their personalities. That's all. They are just us, dead. That's all.

So, I got up and pulled the other dining chairs away from the table and invited them to sit and talk to us. Whilst I sure felt caught between two worlds, and considerably out of my depth, I also knew I could trust my Team to work through this clearing with me. I asked John to light the candles in the centre of the table.

I swallowed and opened my mouth to speak hoping that words would come out. I didn't have a clue what I was doing or saying, so I allowed my Team to do the talking.

"You've been caught out! I can see right through you! You've discovered that you can mess with John's head from

JOHN: FRIGHT NIGHT

the vantage point that you have there. Whilst you might have lived a lowly life when you were on earth, now is the time to begin your Spiritual journey."

One of the entities then spoke up, laughing out loud, "Oh! So you want us to go to this light place? Well, lady, we have no intention of sitting under a light for the rest of our days when we can have way more fun doing what we're doing. Now that we have finished with John, we will just move onto our next victim! Ha! An old lady perhaps!" And they all laughed.

"See, that's where you are wrong. You guys used to love motorbikes and golf and going to bars right? Well, they have them where you are too! You are denying yourself and your Souls the opportunities to develop spiritually. Go and join one of the motorbike groups. The Leaders of these Groups are Spiritual Teachers. Go and join a golf club. The Leaders of these Groups are Spiritual Teachers. Go to the bar and talk to the waitresses. Yes, even the waitresses are Spiritual Teachers. Your days of messing with people's heads are over."

With that, I summoned the Archangel Michael and Archangel Uriel. The spiritual heavyweights, you might say. No words were exchanged. The Archangels simply lifted these guys up and out of their chairs and they all glided away. Somewhat stereotypically, towards a bright light. Without even a look over their shoulders, they were gone. Definitely gone. This time forever.

I came back into the room and looked at John. "WOW!" he said, "That was amazing! Did you feel how cold it was in here? And now it's not? I can't believe what just happened, yet I know it was real. Are you Ok?"

Was I ok? Hmmm, not sure. When I do this work it feels amazing. But coming back into the real world usually means doubting what has happened.

It was when I received John's Testimonial some days later that I knew that we had shared something very significant.

Testimonial from John

It was early 2015, when I felt my life had hit rock bottom. Out of anxiety, I called Marion who offered to see me that day. This is a day I will always remember. The psychometric reading and guidance that Marion gave me that day was simply amazing. A few weeks on, I was being troubled by some unwanted entities during my sleep. Again, I phoned Marion and she offered to call past my house. On her visit, she did a clearing of these entities and I have had no problems since. I have slept like a baby ever since. Further on, I was on holidays in Alice Springs when my life turned upside down again. A text message to Marion was all it took for her to again guide me along the correct path. Marion's counselling, guidance and care is second to none.

Stu: A Happy Sceptic

Dedicated to Stu

Stuart and I have known each other since we were 14. In fact, he asked me to marry him at 16! I never answered him. He moved away the next day to work as a Jackaroo in the country. I never saw him again until about 2 years ago. I used to travel from Perth to Adelaide to visit my parents who had both been really unwell. I wasn't sure how long I still had with Mum and felt it important to come and see her as often as I could for as long as I could.

I would run into Stu at the shops and we would talk about life. He was going through a divorce and had just had a major heart attack, resulting in him having a defibrillator implanted in his chest.

Stu used to drive plant equipment on mine sites around Western Australia and loved what he did. He was proud of all he had achieved for himself work wise, up until the accident that took away his love of plant equipment. That was, until they took his licence away due to his condition.

As a result, he was unemployable. Thinking he may never work again with three children under 16 to support, fear and depression started to creep in.

During our conversation in the November, seven months after his heart attack, he told me that he was worried about his future. He had no savings, no house and had just bought a $2000 car. I tried to cheer him up. I had little emotional support to give as I was giving it all to my parents, but I was able to give him a glimmer of hope to hang onto.

Stu knew I was a Psychic. He thought what I did was weird. He was a firm sceptic. Even so, I got a message for him, which I gave to him, and he's since told me that it got him through many dark moments of self-doubt.

"Stu, enjoy the summer here on Lake Alexandrina with your kids. I can confidently reassure you that you will get a job. You will apply for a job soon and on the second Friday in February, you'll get it. I promise. Hold on for it. It will happen. Just go sailing and canoeing this summer and enjoy your time reconnecting with your kids. You've worked the FIFO (fly in fly out) lifestyle for ten years. It's time for you all to get to know each other again. You have a second chance."

I knew this message was true, and on the second Friday in February so did Stuart. My mobile phone rang on my desk at work on the second Friday in February, 4 months after my premonition. I hadn't heard from Stu since our conversation in the November, but recognised his voice instantly when I answered the phone. He was ecstatic,

STU: A HAPPY SCEPTIC

"Marion, Marion, I got the job just like you said I would!"

"What do you mean?" I asked him. I'd actually forgotten the message I'd given him months earlier.

"Today is the second Friday in February and my new employer has just rung me to tell me I was the successful applicant for the job. Remember? That's what you told me would happen. Back in November. You said I would hear that I got the job on the second Friday in February. I still think what you do is weird, but I'm glad you were right about this! I did make the most of summer with the kids. Part of me must have trusted your prediction. Hey and guess what? I also get a company car!"

Well, fancy that.

Riley: Triple N

Dedicated to Riley and Grace

Hearing anguish and desperation from the other end of the phone when talking to a Mum is scary. My instinct is to help, my fear is that I can't.

In January 2016 I received a Facebook message from Grace. She said that she'd read my blurb on Facebook and was worried for her 17 year old son. I rang her as soon as I'd finished reading her message.

After explaining all about myself she said, "Well, actually I was thinking of coming to see you myself but now I'm wondering if you would see my 17 year old son?"

"Sure, what's going on?" I asked.

"My son was in year 11 last year. He's struggled with mental health for some time, and has developed a drug habit. Midway through the last term he refused to leave his room except to go to his part time job to get money for drugs. Every time I ask him to come out of his room, he threatens to kill me or kill himself. He's violent and hostile. He's sees Psychologists, a Psychiatrist and Counsellors but none of it seems to help. He refuses to take his medication."

"Grace, talk to him. If he wants to come to see me, I'd like to meet him. It needs to be his choice though."

While I'd been talking to Grace, I started a new page in my Reading notebook and wrote down the names Nathan and Siena.

Grace rang me back later that morning and asked when my next available appointment would be. I told her that I'd in fact had a cancellation for 3pm that very afternoon.

At 3pm, Grace and Riley arrived. Grace with her smile, Riley with his typical 17 year old attitude. I invited them to sit. Grace faced me, Riley turned away from me.

"Thank you Grace, for bringing Riley to see me this afternoon," I said. "Riley, thank you for coming to see me. What did your Mum tell you about me?" I asked.

Riley responded with, "She said you were some kind of psychic or spiritual person. Prove it!" Gotta love kids with attitude.

"Ok. I've got two names for you," I said, "Nathan and Siena."

Riley flipped his head around and growled at his mum, "Why did you tell her about them?"

"I didn't. I don't even know who they are!" replied his Mum.

"Yeah, so what do you know about them then?" he asked.

"Well, I know that Nathan is a 23 year old boy that

you work with. Actually, you can learn from him. He has a very good work ethic. You like him. He knows how to give people what they want so he gets what he wants. Watch him and you will go a long way. Siena is a girl you will one day have a very special relationship with. Now, would you like to stay and talk to me or would you like to leave now with your Mum?"

I could see that Grace was hoping Riley would stay, which he did. Whilst Riley barely looked at me during the first half hour of what turned out to be a two and a half hour appointment, I did feel the ice thaw. Luckily, ice is transparent, so I could see straight through him.

I had given Riley enough proof for the first Reading and let him talk and talk and talk for the remaining time. It wasn't a Reading as such. But I did connect to Riley straight away. I silently hoped that I could one day get him to see the future he held in his hands but couldn't see at the moment.

Riley and Grace went home that day and things went quite well for a few days, I understand.

Then I received a phone call from Grace asking if she could bring Riley back as he wanted another session with me. This time, I wrote down the name Natalie in my book.

Grace just dropped him off this time and he came in and sat himself down, focused on the same spot on the wall as he had been last time.

"What name have you got for me this week then smarty?" asked Riley.

"Natalie," I said.

"Yeah, so what do you know about her?"

"I know that she's someone you admire and is involved in the kind of work you are interested in. Am I right?"

"How do you know these things?" he said as he got out his phone to show me some text messages. "Look, I was texting her this morning. She's good for me. She helps me. She's one of my Teacher's at school and I get on really well with her."

"I get the sense that she's interested in plants or nature in some big way, like you."

"That's right," said Riley, "She used to be a Ranger and that's what I'd like to be. She's the only teacher at school I like and she's helping me to find a traineeship in Horticulture."

"Perfect," I said, "That's exactly what you need to be involved in."

Riley and I then went into quite an involved discussion about what he saw as his role in the world. I also told him what I saw his role as. They were the same. From there we went into quite an involved discussion about his spiritual journey and life at home with his Mum.

Riley then asked me the following question, "How come I can talk to you? I'm in the CAMS Mental Health system. I have Counsellors and Psychologists and I can't talk to any of them. Why is that? Why do I feel connected to you and that you understand me?"

Tough one to answer, but I gave it a shot, "Riley, there certainly is a place in our society for these professionals. However, I feel that they stick a label on you and put you in a box that they've studied about and understood from their text books. They work on your mind. To me, that's too hard. I can't work with the mind. I have my own issues with my own mind. The mind's too complicated for me. I work on a very deep, but simple, Soul level. At our most basic, we're all just souls that want to love and be loved. Simple."

Riley understood and accepted the explanation. I told Riley that I had been shown an amazing image of him as a Wizard standing on top of the world as a globe, reaching down into the darkness and pulling trees out of black planets, making them healthy and sunny again. I saw him do this to hundreds of planets, never taking his feet off earth. I wish I could have downloaded that image for Riley as I feel that if he saw it he would realise his own potential.

Riley was indeed an Old Soul that had been here many times before. That's why he was struggling with life, because he knew how straight forward life could be. He didn't want to be involved in all the mind games and emotional blackmail that people played at their lower levels.

Riley was a misfit. He felt like he didn't belong. He was a very gifted soul; caught between two worlds, much like I was. Always taking things personally, wondering why people couldn't just get on with life and not get bogged down with insignificant problems.

Riley may have been an old soul, but he wasn't really a wise one. Not yet, anyway. That would come and it would come with hardship. Nothing worth achieving is ever easy. Like everyone else in this world, Riley would have to keep learning his lessons, as we all have to.

Sadly, his expectations for this life seemed to be incongruous with reality. He seemed to think he was immune from having to learn anything. His attitude of expectancy was an issue. He expected jobs to just be offered to him. And not just any jobs, ones that made him a lot of money for as little an effort as possible. That day, as he left and his eyes held mine, I think I saw a thank you hiding in there.

It was a couple of weeks before I saw Riley again. I'd emailed him the notes of his Readings so that he could refer to them. His Mum and I kept in constant contact. She was so frightened of losing her son. So much so that I feared she was pushing him away. In reality, she was simply pushing him closer to independence.

A while later, Grace told me that Riley was back at school and undertaking Year 12. He'd booked into a Certificate course in Horticulture and was looking at getting work experience in a local community nursery. The relationship between her son and herself had really improved and Riley had in fact inspired Grace to work out her own demons. Life was going ok.

Riley came to see me a few weeks later. This time, he looked me in the eye from the time he sat down to the time he left.

"Ok, what have you got for me today?" he asked.

"I get the word naturalist today. You are a naturalist. You will be instrumental in plant research and also research around legalising medical cannabis. You have the opportunity to become a Park Ranger."

Riley punched the air at this point with a big smile on his face, "Yippee!"

"No, medical cannabis," I emphasised.

Riley and I had enjoyed some deep conversations about the meaning of life and Spirituality and his role in both. But I needed his attention now.

"Riley, the first week you came to see me I gave you the name Nathan, the first three letters of which are nat. The second week I gave you the name Natalie, which follows the same pattern. This visit I've told you you're going to be a naturalist. Are you seeing the link here? They're all signposts. You can't tell me that you are not meant to be here."

When Grace came to pick him up after our session, Riley stood at the stairs at the bottom of the deck. Again, his eyes locked into mine and through his tears I felt like he was pleading with me to deliver him straight to the end point of his journey. Of course, I couldn't do that. This was his journey, and his alone.

Whilst Riley was an old soul, he was also a 17 year old wanting the world to recognize him and his uniqueness, as so many 17 year olds strive for. He still had a lot to learn, but he now understands that he is caught between two worlds and needs to learn to balance them both.

Riley did well for a while, however, his frustrating domestic situation got the better of him and he paid the price with visits from the police and time in the children's mental health unit at the Children's Hospital.

On his return from hospital, his mum pleaded with me to see him again. This time, I noticed a really big difference in his demeanour. I had seen this look before in my son's eyes (see story about my son). Riley now had entities attached to him.

I really shouldn't use the word entities. After all, these were people. Bad sorts while alive, and now bad sorts above the clouds. They've realised that they can mess with our kids' minds and be very destructive. Perhaps energies is a better term.

I told Riley what I thought the score was and asked him a few questions to clarify exactly what had been going on for him since our last visit. Whilst, I was able to clear these negative energies, I was struggling to help Riley dig himself out of the hole he had chosen to dig and fill in over himself.

I will happily help anyone, but they must be prepared to help themselves. No one changes unless they want to. Spiritual values will help us navigate our lives, but our human ego and mind can be extremely destructive to our growth; often hampering our very best intentions with outbursts of extreme anger, blame and self-delusion.

A few months ago, I heard from Riley. He had moved to northern New South Wales. He was still unemployed, but told me he had been contemplating his future more carefully. Whilst sitting by a creek one day, a box floated past. Actually, he said it didn't float past, it kept circling in front of him. In his own words:

"I was at Rainbow Retreat in Nimbin, down this creek bed just under the bridge that you cross over in order to get to the Retreat. I was sitting on this big concrete slab that crossed over this one section of the creek. I was sitting right at the end where it was cut in half with my friend Kat on my right and Jake next to her. I was gazing out into this big pondy bit of the creek where there were hell whirl pools and all, and then I happened to look over my left shoulder down the creek and noticed this black box floating towards me down stream. I just ignored it, before I knew it I saw this box float right past my leg and I grabbed it out the water, looked at it for a moment and let it go. Next thing, I was walking down the creek bed and saw this rock with the name Siena written on it!"

Riley was desperate to know why he was finding items with the name I gave him at our very first meeting? He wanted me to tell him. He wanted me to break the surprise. But I couldn't. Siena was his present to unwrap, one day in his future. I pray for him daily.

Testimonial from Grace

Hi peeps! A friend has asked me to share a testimony on Marion's Facebook page in regards to her amazing work, healing and demon clearing. A friend took her teenage son (who we will call Sam for this post) to see Marion as she had nowhere else to turn. Sam seemed depressed lost and clostrophobic with life and refused mainstream help and therapy. However on his first therapy session with Marion made a instant connection. On Sams second visit to Marion it was established he had 3 demons attached. One being from Sams grandfather who was killed by a drunk teenage driver 2 years before Sam was born as well as 2 other lost random teenage spirits. Marion cleared these attached spirits and Sam is now finding his path in life with more clarity and direction and a purpose to live again. There is still work needed to be done but Sam is getting there following his path to where he feels he needs to be. I cannot highly recommended Marion enough, she knows her stuff and is truly a gifted, caring special lady and a new friend in my life xx.

Six Beautiful Vietnamese

Dedicated to Mary and Jolene

Mary contacted me to come and Read for her and her girlfriends. When I first met with Mary, my breath was taken away by her exquisite beauty and grace. I'm not only talking about physical beauty, although she has that in spades. I'm also talking about her inner beauty. Whilst Mary was perfectly capable of conducting psychic Readings herself, it's always nice to get someone else in to Read.

Reading yourself would be like a dentist trying to pull their own teeth. Or a Hairdresser trying to cut her own hair, especially the back. We all need someone to go to as it's sometimes just too hard to work on ourselves.

Mary had been trying to synchronise times in order to fit everyone in for their hour long Reading. Jolene proved the hardest to pin down. But of course, my Team had told me that Jolene was the one who needed the Reading the most.

I rescheduled twice in order to accommodate Jolene. I

SIX BEAUTIFUL VIETNAMESE

told Mary that I felt she really needed her Reading. She told me that Jolene had never had one before. On the day we finally settled on, Jolene was last on the list of 6. She still wasn't sure if she would be able to make it. I sincerely hoped she would.

These beautiful girls were all from Vietnam. At the end of the night, when all the Readings were done, we'd planned for Mary to prepare the most amazing smorgasbord of fresh vegetables and salad. I was quite looking forward to that! As it happened, they taught me how to make authentic cold spring rolls.

When I arrived, I was greeted by a beautifully set up room complete with six floor cushions, fresh frangipanis on each, and candles. The room had a beautiful energy.

Each of the women were exquisite. In looks, personality and mannerisms. It was really interesting for me to Read women from a totally different culture. All of them brought along photographs and questions pertinent for them at that point in time. They also brought their own insight and stories to share. Gosh, I love what I do!

In the course of her Reading, I gave Mary the name Stefan as a connection for her. I also told her that if she was currently thinking about Nursing as a career, then she'd made the right choice! She confirmed that Stefan was her boyfriend and she'd just completed her application for Nursing. She was very happy to receive confirmation that both were meant to be in her life.

The moment Loan was seated in front of me for her Reading, I asked her, "Who in your family has a secret? I sense that it is your Mum. I also see bars and sense that it's not a secret that has made the family happy." Loan's Mum was in prison. Greed had got the better of her. Her family were devastated.

Several other profound messages came through for these girls as the afternoon wore on, but I was conscious that Jolene still hadn't shown up. She was late. That was ok, I knew her Dad would wait.

Jolene had never had a Reading before. She'd always been too scared. I reassured her that even though she had never had a Reading before, I had done plenty and asked her to trust me to deliver any messages to her with friendship and compassion.

Due to the language barrier, Jolene's dad could only show me the letter 'L' with his hands, to indicate his name starting with the letter L. Jolene confirmed that her Dad's name was Leng. I also saw that Jolene's dad had a lot of sunspots on his face, identifying him immediately.

Jolene was shocked. But it was when I told her that her Dad was looking at me with his hands over his heart, downcast eyes and an apologetic expression that Jolene knew in herself that this was a real message from her Dad.

I never found out what Jolene's dad was sorry for, but I know that knowing he was meant a lot to her. And that's why I do this.

The Lesson

Despite cultural differences, Spirit will always find a

way to give those I Read for exactly what they need. Even though English is a universal language, so is sign language. It was sign language from Spirit that got the message through on numerous occasions that afternoon.

June: Geraldton in Wartime

Dedicated to June, Chas and Sam

On 11 November 2015 (11.11.2015) I was invited to do a Psychic Reading for a lovely woman named June Rose who lives in Encounter Bay, South Australia. I had never met June before and only spoke with her briefly the week before to make the appointment and to take her address.

On arrival at June's home, I was warmly welcomed and invited to take a seat on a lounge. June went to the kitchen to make morning tea. As I sat on the lounge, a small Gentleman in a tight, strict blue uniform with a hat sat next to me. The uniform looked to be of military style.

"Hi," I said to the Gentleman.

"Hello," he replied.

I said to him, "Do you know June?" To which he replied, "Yes, I do".

"May I ask your name and connection to June please?" I asked him.

JUNE: GERALDTON IN WARTIME

"My name is Charles Patching but June would know me as Chas. That was how her father knew me. I was her father's best friend. June feels like a daughter to me. I never had a daughter."

The feeling of love that came through Chas' visit was like no other love I had ever felt before. It filled me from head to toe. I was covered in goose bumps.

I was surprised at how quickly Chas had appeared. I turned to check if June would be much longer, naturally I was eager to tell her about her guest, but when I turned back to talk to Chas, he had gone.

It was at this point that June walked in and saw a look of bewilderment on my face. She asked if I was ok, to which I replied, "Yes, but I think you've just had your first guest for today."

June sat quietly and listened as I explained Chas' visit. Her eyes filled with tears. She told me the story about the relationship between Charlie 'Chas' Patching and her father Clarence 'Sam' Rose. Charles Patching was her Dad's best friend, she confirmed. They were in the Air Force together, based at Pearce Air Base (WA). At one point during World War II, Clarence had just flown five marine coast watch missions in a row. When he landed at Geraldton Air Base, his Lieutenant told him he had to go up again. His best friend, Chas, said to him, "Let me do this one mate." The two of them agreed to flip a coin. Chas won the toss.

The flight left Geraldton Airport at 05:57 am on 15 March 1943. Unfortunately, the plane struck heavy fog and turned around to return to the airport. The pilot, Donald Ashby Waite, had misread the valleys on their map and soon after, the plane smashed into a hilltop ridge at Yetna, Geraldton.

All eight men on board perished that morning. Sam joined the team assigned to pick up the remains of his best mate and crew.

June said to me, "Marion, do you know what day it is today?"

"Thursday," I said.

Smiling she said, "No, it's the 11th of the 11th. It's Remembrance Day! Look at the time - 11:00am. This is the time we remember our lost soldiers. I would not be here today if it had not been for Chas flying on behalf of my Dad that day. My father telegrammed me in November every year to ask me to remember and honour his best friend on that Day. Today is also my Dad's birthday."

This felt very special, if somewhat surreal. How wonderful that Chas came through as proof of life after death for June that morning. It gave her the kind of comfort and closure that she'd never been able to experience before.

June said, "Marion, there's one regret I have in life and that is that I will never get to lay flower's on Chas's grave. It makes me so sad."

"June," I said, "I will find out where they are and do this for you on your behalf. It will be my honour."

Together with June's help, we contacted the War Museum in Canberra who gave us all the details of that fateful flight and the crew on board. They put me in touch

JUNE: GERALDTON IN WARTIME

with the Geraldton Museum and Mr Robert Bandy. It was Robert's job to lay memorial plaques at all of the crash sites around Geraldton. Many years ago, there was a flying training school in Geraldton and consequently, many crashes.

When I rang Robert to ask him if he had any details or knowledge about the crash on 15 March 1943 at Yetna, he told me he knew it well as it had been written in a local history book about the area. I told Robert I was coming to Geraldton and would like to meet with him. He agreed to meet us and said he would even take us to the crash site.

It's nice to think about simply going where life leads you. In my line of work, I really have no choice. That's the only way I know how to live. It's not always comfortable, but it's often exceptionally rewarding. This was one of those times. I had gone from June's Reading, speaking to Chas, to visiting his crash site. My life is weird, but most certainly wonderful. I knew this was a completely new chapter in my life as a Psychic Medium. This was no longer my imagination, it was real.

I visited Geraldton together with my best friend Jennifer in February 2016. We met with Mr Robert Bandy, Historian at the local Geraldton Museum. Robert had been instrumental in locating and mapping the majority of the plane crashes that occurred in and around Geraldton and Northampton for the Historical Society. He had actually pegged the site of the A9173 crash some years prior in the hope that someday a plaque could be erected in memory of those that lost their lives. To date, that plaque does not exist.

Robert showed us a book entitled The RAAF Historical Record of No 4 Service Flying Training School. On page 257 of that book, Robert showed us two photographs of the crashed Beaufort Bomber on top of the ridge at Yetna. There is a short description alongside the photographs and a Record Log of the flight on the next page. To see the photographs was quite chilling. This Reading was becoming more real than any before.

Robert kindly took us the 20 minute drive to a remote, harshly landscaped hilltop just east of Yetna. We climbed the hillside to arrive at the staked site surrounded by shards of metal and burnt Perspex shrapnel. Robert picked up some pieces of shrapnel and handed them to me saying I could keep them and to give some to June back in Victor Harbor, South Australia.

Robert, Jennifer and I all walked off in various directions absorbed in our own thoughts and prayers. I took myself off to an area where I could absorb the energies of those whose lives perished on that hilltop. It's in trying to describe moments like this that my words fail me worst. I couldn't begin to describe my feelings on that hilltop in Yetna.

I quietly prayed for those lost Souls and their families that never got to grow old with them. I honoured their souls and sacrifices on that remote cliff that day on behalf of their families.

Back in SA, I bought a heart shaped box and took the

pieces of shrapnel around to June on the first day of my return. She was overwhelmed.

This whole experience was quite a journey for me. I know that my best friend, Jennifer, also felt the gravity of what we were doing there that day. There are simply no words to describe the emotion and honour we both felt.

I can't say with any scientific exactness that June's reading proved the existence of an afterlife. I guess it all comes down to whether you believe that I actually saw Chas or not. June's testimony should be enough to show you that I knew nothing about her before arriving at her house. And let's face it, people who have actually gone mad don't usually provide such specific and relevant information.

Testimonial from June

Dear Marion, how truly beautiful and so clever you are. The dedication, the accuracy of names, and how amazing to know Charles Patching really was able to heal by connecting. I thank my late father for all the information given to me throughout the years. Of course, as children we cannot possibly fathom the extent of pain and suffering our parents go through.

I am so proud to know you Marion, your Higher Self must truly amaze so so many. I sincerely wish you so much love, happiness and true success with all your endeavours throughout life. How loyal, true and honest you were with all your spoken words. No one else knew anything about this. It was all information entrusted only to me by my Father. Kindest and richest blessings Marion, Love, June Rose.

A Collection of Short Stories

My family and friends have always referred to my premonitions and the way I just know things as 'weird stuff'. Sometimes I just know stuff. I used to question why I needed to know. Nowadays though, in the lighthearted moments, I treat it as fun. Sometimes it gives me shortcuts to situations or issues, which comes in handy.

Sometimes the information is so factual and real that I cannot ignore it no matter how hard I try. On these occasions, it's always for the better.

In this section, I will share a whole lot of different Psychic experiences that people have told me about during their Readings. Things they have experienced for themselves. My hope is that it will help you recognise for yourself exactly how random knowledge can be and that you should never discount it as being just your imagination. It might be. But it's equally possible that there's a message that you really need to hear.

I recommend that you buy a notebook and start making a note of dreams or visions that you have. Date, time, scenario, outcome etc. In the meantime, may these short stories help build your awareness and confidence of the fact that our intuition, higher self or Soul knows way more than the mind.

Theresa

Theresa was a beautiful girl, I was taken with her appearance at once. She was someone that made not judging a book by its cover difficult. But she was proof of why that's never a good idea as the contents were nothing like the cover when it came to Theresa.

She was a methamphetamine addict and had given birth to a son 6 months before I met her. She knew she had to stop using. She believed in Angels and Guides. What she didn't believe in was herself.

She had been asking for help but hadn't been listening. Her Angels had been trying to help her but somehow the screaming baby always took priority. So, they sent her to me.

Theresa had taken meth right through her pregnancy, the birth and right up until the day she saw me. She admitted that other people had to take care of her son because sometimes she would sleep for days and then would be up for days while using.

She begged me for help. I gave her the spiel that you've no doubt become familiar with by now, "Theresa, today is one day." I told her that I could see two baby girls waiting for her to be their Mum. Suddenly it hit home, she had to stop. She heard them too. Finally there was room inside her head for them to get through. Thank God.

A few days after I saw her, she emailed me this testimonial:

"Hi Marion. I loved my reading. It gave me a sense of relief and I was calm for the first time in almost a year. I sat by the water and read your Reading and just sobbed. I took my time driving home and even stopped in Strathalbyn to get some herbs and flowers for my garden. My partner was almost in tears reading your report. I agree that I need professional counselling ASAP, maybe even an anger management class. I get frustrated too easily and say nasty things I don't mean. I still believe a negative spirit is with me, not as strong, but it's still here. My partner would like to meet you and get some reiki and guidance, so hopefully we will meet again soon. A sincere thank you for helping me believe in myself."

Tracey

I was invited to Read for Tracey in the beautiful Adelaide Hills town of Mount Barker. Tracey had never had a Reading before, but saw my blurb on the Facebook community pages and her interest was piqued.

Before I arrived at Tracey's, I had actually written down a lot of the information for her in my book. I asked her if she would like to hear what I had written down. She said, "Yes, because my friend told me I am not to tell you anything!"

Goodo, testing the Psychic again.

I gave Tracey a description of both her sons, knowing the eldest loved basketball and the other loved the stage and singing. I also asked her if she had lost someone's special penny once? Then I told her that when she was a little girl she was scared of clowns.

"How do you know all that?" she asked in wonder.

"Well, I guess I must be Psychic," I said facetiously.

"OK, wow, that's awesome. What else do you know?"

"I know that you work in a car dealership and that you don't like your boss." I described him to her physically. His mannerisms, super ego and all.

"Wow! That's simply amazing. All that without me telling you anything! You certainly do have a Gift."

We spent another hour in Tracey's Reading, until I asked a final question, "Tracey, do you have any other questions you would like to ask me before we finish up?"

"Yes! How do I get rid of my boss?"

Can't tell you the rest.

Crystal

Crystal came to me with one question, "How can I get in touch with my Guides?" She explained that she was having real anger issues and controlling her emotions. We talked about this for a while.

I asked Crystal if she could relate to a little baby boy named Ashley.

"Yes!" she exclaimed and promptly started crying, "Ashley was my baby boy that I lost when I was still pregnant."

Whoa.

I might just interject here and tell you what it feels like for me when I do Readings like this. I keep forgetting to tell you about what's going on for me. All I'm doing is giving information. But being able to provide Mums a reconnection with babies they have lost, that's special. You can imagine it fills me with incredible emotion and love.

If you've ever been in love, well, that's the feeling I get when Spirits come through me to make a connection. It's extremely difficult to put into words. I feel like nothing else in the world matters except that person, just like being in love.

For the time I receive messages for whomever I'm reading for, I fall in love. I feel like everything is right in the world.

Anyway, back to Crystal.

"Crystal, Ashley would like you to go to the beach where you will find a shell. It will be a shell like you haven't seen before. Ashley wants you to pick it up and take it home. Every time you feel stressed, he's asked me to ask you to hold it, as he can help you now that he's an Angel."

Claudia

Claudia rang me from interstate for a phone Reading, she wanted to talk relationships. I wanted to talk to Claudia about health check-ups of the female variety. Which we did, thank goodness.

Claudia rang me six months later to thank me for focusing on health rather than the loser boyfriend she'd had. I had been insistent that she go have her regular pap smear. She hadn't had one for many years. In fact, she couldn't even remember the last time.

Claudia's test came back with abnormal cells. She was monitored over a period of time and given a clean bill of health. Because of my advice, she had her daughter tested too. Her daughter's tests also came back with abnormal cells and she was given chemotherapy. Thankfully, the disease was caught in time.

Ladies, never delay your mammograms or pap smears. Get them over and done with. They're on your mind anyway, taking up precious space that you could be using to relax. Book the appointment for yourself and your daughters today. Remember, someday never comes.

Tenielle

Tenielle was very spiritually aware. She worked in a local new age store, understood karma and practiced gratitude. But she felt she just wasn't getting anywhere with her husband.

I arrived at Tenielle's on a grey, autumn day. As soon as I walked into the house, I cringed. Something was very wrong in that house.

"Tenielle, I'm sorry, but I can't Read for you," I said. "My head's all furry and I'm not making any sense to myself. Is this your house? Have you lived here long? I feel like someone that used to live here before you has left behind some very negative energy. Were they drug dealers perhaps or did they use a lot of drugs? I feel like there's a big secret here."

Tenielle suggested we sit outside. Once we were outside in the fresh air, the Reading floated freely like it normally does. "I'm so sorry, I couldn't get anything for you inside."

"Marion, you asked me about the history of this house. Well, we have only been in this house two years. The people who owned it before were drug dealers. But most importantly, the secret that you picked up on was that of my husband's. He is a drug dealer and is stoned most of the time, even at work. His family doesn't know about his addiction, only I do. I've begged him to get counselling and stop for the sake of our three young daughters. He just won't listen to me. He's angry all the time and occasionally violent towards us. All we do is fight. I don't want our girls to see us fighting anymore. Marion, how can I get him to stop?"

"Leave him," I said.

Imogen

I liked Imogen immediately. Her Reading was very special in many ways. But, in one way in particular. During the morning, Imogen's daughter came in to the room. I had never seen a real life Angel, but I did that morning. Oh My Goodness!

"You're just beautiful!" I thought to myself when I

looked at this little girl with dark curly hair and big, deep dark brown eyes.

"My name's Carla," she said, through her thoughts.

At the exact same time, Imogen said to her, "Carla, please say hallo to Marion."

"You are very special," was the thought I sent back to her.

"I'm Mummy's Teacher," was the thought I received back.

"What are you here to teach Mummy?" I asked, again through my thoughts.

"How to love people and how to forgive people. Can I go play now?"

I was speechless. All I could do was nod my head. Imogen then said to me, "Did she just communicate with you telepathically?"

"Yes," I said.

"She does that all the time with me," said Imogen.

The world is so out of balance. Who better to put the world back in shape than beautiful children like Carla. My Team showed me that day how this is being done right here, right now. Children are the key to the future of our world. They live in their souls 100% of the time. We teach them to ignore the soul and listen to the mind. If only we'd let them teach us.

Our souls are simple. They just want to love and be loved. Our minds are complicated.

I say bring more children into the world to touch our lives. Over the years, many families have experienced the extreme heartache of losing a child. Whether it be through natural loss or through a decision not to have the baby, these children are being reincarnated almost immediately into the lives of new families leaving behind their original families forever changed.

Children come into our lives for a reason. They awaken incredibly complex and deep emotions within us. The love of a child can only be felt. It cannot be described. Equally, the loss of a child can only be felt. I can never be described.

Children are bringing the world back into balance one family at a time, starting with yours. Next time, you look into the eyes of a child think, "You're an old soul," trust that feeling. Seek to learn from that child.

Amelia

Life had been an intense journey for Amelia. She's a drummer and plays with bands around the coastal area in South Australia. She uses drums as meditation, healing and stress relief.

I knew that when Amelia called me for help, she really needed it and was ready to receive it. She was eager to learn and listened with her whole being. Everything I said seemed to resonate deeply with her. I saw through her pain to a woman worthy of loving and living.

Amelia had bi-polar disease. It's a hideous illness. I know, I have it. Just another way I feel caught between two worlds.

Amelia asked me for a Reiki session. So I packed up

the portable bed, and headed to her house for the morning with my Team. I'm glad we did.

Amelia hadn't been drumming recently and was struggling with her bi-polar. During the session, I felt a pair of hands lay over mine. They came with love so I knew it was alright to trust.

"Welcome," I said to whoever belonged to these hands.

"I'm Brendan," he said, "Please tell Amelia, to start drumming on my kit again. Tell her, I will sit on her shoulder and help her. Tell her I'm glad she bought my drum kit. She's an awesome drummer!"

And with that he was gone. I simply had to interrupt the Reiki, as I knew the message would go a long way towards Amelia's healing. She immediately confirmed that she had bought the drum kit from Brendan's father who was selling it because Brendan had passed away. She was thrilled that he came through to her that day and that he approved of the way she drummed on his drum kit!

When I left Amelia that day, she was eager to pick up her sticks and dedicate her first song to Brendan. And the next. And the next.

Melissa

Love doesn't need words. I say that often. I feel like Melissa's reading was a great example of it.

The name Grace came through very quickly at Melissa's Reading. I knew it was because I could speak the words she wanted Melissa to hear. Grace was still alive, but had dementia and no longer spoke.

"Tell Melissa that she's wonderful and I wish to thank her for all she's done for me. I can't talk but I need her to know that before I go." I sensed that Grace may decide to pass during the next 24-48 hours and it was vital I gave Melissa that message.

Melissa worked as an aged carer. She is the type of person I would want caring for me as I age. Because it was easy to tell that she really did care.

As Humans we have jobs to do, but equally, as Souls we have jobs to do. As a carer, Melissa was certainly in the right place career. I could tell that by the amount of visitors that had lined up to say hi and thank her for the care she had given them. There was Jenny, Henry, Grace, Matthew, Daniel, Mark and Joan. Joan, too, like Grace, couldn't speak and merely held up a picture of a heart.

Melissa didn't receive any visits from relatives that day. But she did receive lots of visits from family. There's a difference. Think about it.

We are born into families, but that doesn't necessarily mean we fit into them. I admire anyone that wishes to spend their life as a Carer. I can't image how tough it is getting close to people that you know are in God's Waiting Room. The feelings and emotions shared between carers and their patients can be very intense. Sadly, as a result, some carers don't get to experience these emotions in their own family lives. They, too, feel caught between two worlds.

CAUGHT BETWEEN TWO WORLDS

Tallara

To say Tallara was spirited is an understatement. The girl was a Dynamo! She romped into my house with the biggest smile I've ever seen. I liked her immediately. She was blessed with an incredible amount of infectious energy, wit and vivaciousness.

Tallara was pure Soul. Unsurprisingly, she was blessed with an incredible amount of significant contacts ready and waiting to welcome her to her first ever Reading. Let me see, there was Enid, Yvonne, George, Brian, Laurie, Steph, Bill, Gloria and Anthony. Turns out that Anthony and Gloria were actually related. Tallara knew each and every one of her guests that day, telling me little anecdotes about each of them.

I told Tallara that I saw her surrounded by children's books and children as if she was at a book launch! Then I realised that she was the author and I described the vision further. The colours, the laughter and the joy, as well as the admiration of Tallara's Mum standing off to the side.

Tallara squealed with delight saying that that's exactly what she'd been working on and the fact that I saw a book launch delighted her, "Ooh, how exciting! Thank you!"

Tallara had also come with a list of questions, most of which I answered before she even asked them, which she thought was incredibly clever. She even asked me if I could teach her the trick! Her main question was, "What is the likelihood of me getting the grade point average I need to do Honours?"

I replied "Professor Tallara, you will surprise them all, even yourself!"

Her second question was, "Will I be able to cope with doing Honours?"

I replied, "Well, I'll describe it this way. After winter, our feet are usually very sensitive and the first time we walk on the hot sand at the beach in summer, our feet really can't cope with it. But if we go to the beach every day to walk on the hot sand, our feet get tougher. We train them to get used to the pain and by the end of summer we don't feel it. Soon enough, we can't even remember what that pain was like. That's what doing Honours will be like for you."

Tallara liked that analogy as she loved the beach. I recommended to Tallara's Mum, who had come along for a Reading also, that she stock up on: chocolate, salt and vinegar chips and jars of peanut butter!

Neil and Simon

Sometimes kids that are being bullied wish that something would magically happen to help them in their situations. And whilst I am always caught between two worlds fighting with myself as to whether or not the information I receive is accurate and whether or not I should pass it on, I'm glad I did on this occasion.

I was at a party one day and I saw a kid, a teenager. I wasn't even sure who he belonged to at the party. But I knew my Team would guide me to the rightful recipients of the messages that were coming through.

About an hour and a half later, I found myself in a discussion with five other people. They were mostly talking amongst themselves. I turned to the guy next to me, whose name I later learned was Neil, and asked him if he had a nephew named Simon that went to (school name withheld)? He said, "Yes I do, how do you know him?"

I told him straight out that I feared that Simon was being bullied badly at school and really needed to get out of the school that he was in as a matter of urgency. I felt it was life and death, so I asked if he would be able to help? I explained how I knew and apologised to him, fearing he was a sceptic.

"Simon, is my nephew. I haven't heard whether he is being bullied at school but I will certainly find out and yes I will help him. See that couple over there, they are Simon's parents. It's really good that you came to me to tell me about their Son, because if you had told them, they would have just scoffed at you and probably walked away. Thanks for the info, I'll follow it up." With that, we parted ways.

Five years later, I was at a girlfriend's party when Neil came up to me.

"Hi, I don't know if you remember me, but I remember you. I want to thank you for telling me about Simon being bullied at school. We had no idea. The bullying was really bad and Simon had in fact been thinking about taking his own life in order to get out of the situation. I spoke with my brother and his wife. They then spoke with Simon who verified everything. They transferred Simon out of that school and into a new one the same day. I don't know what would have happened to Simon if you hadn't have given me your message. My brother and his wife were thankful as well. I think it may have even opened their eyes to some things. Again, thank you."

Barb

When I returned Barb's phone call, I found it difficult to resist making the time to see her that same day as she requested. She clearly needed my help. I was way over the other side of the city, but my Team encouraged me to drive the hour to get to see Barb.

Barb, I guessed, was approximately 70. She was forthright, warm and delightful. We just clicked. I love it when that happens. "I need to get out of this place but I just can't seem to," she told me.

"I'm so miserable here, it just doesn't feel like home to me at all. I've tried selling, I've tried looking for a new place but nothing's happening. I just can't get out of here. Please tell me I'm not going to be here forever. I'm getting so down. I just don't like this environment anymore. The people are negative and I just don't fit. I'm miserable. Please tell me I am going to get out of here soon."

Immediately, I pointed in the direction of a unit across the way and said, "There's a dark haired lady that lives there, you need to help her. Until you do that, you can't move. Your Soul chose to help her."

"Oh, that's Pat!" Barb exclaimed, "She's lovely".

"Barb, Pat is lovely, but she's also extremely lonely. You'd never know it to look at her. You need to check in on her this week, maybe invite her for a coffee? She would be ever so grateful."

"Oh, that makes sense. Yes, of course, I can do that. I always send her love. I feel she needs it. 'Pat,' I say 'sending you love.'"

"Barb, I have a Daphne here and she would like to confirm the message I just gave you about Pat."

Barb covered her eyes to hide her tears. I reached out to her and held her hand.

"Daphne was my best friend. We used to ride our bikes together after work. We were such good friends. She knew me so well. We had such fun together. I miss her so much," she said.

"Barb, Daphne wants you to remember the person you were when she knew you. She would also like you to bring out a photo of her and keep it close by so you won't feel so lonely. Will you do that for her?"

"Yes," she said, "I will."

Mum Wants The Last Word

Sandra rang me to make a booking. The whole time I was talking on the phone, I had an older lady with greying curly hair insist to me that I was talking to her "Deidre".

I politely told her that I was talking to Sandra and asked would she please give us some privacy.

When Sandra arrived for her appointment a week later, the older lady came to visit again, clapping excitedly all the while squealing, "That's my Deidre, that's my Deidre!"

I again asked her politely to respect our privacy, which I thought she had done.

During the Reading however, she was sitting behind me looking at Sandra with love in her eyes and heart, saying, "Oh that's my Deidre, that's my Deidre."

I mentioned to Sandra what had been happening.

Sandra laughed and said, "Oh, that's my Mum, she wanted to call me Deidre but my Dad didn't like the name and they called me Sandra instead."

Once acknowledged, Mum was happy to move on. Finally at peace.

PART THREE:
Advice

Soul Food

"The Soul knows more than the mind."

When people come to see me for a Reading, I always prepare a special morning or afternoon tea. I light candles and play beautiful background music. I welcome them as a friend. I ask them to leave their human selves at the door as we will just be talking Soul to Soul.

I always like to find out where they sit in relation to their own Spiritual Journey. I ask them if they believe in Souls, or that we are here to learn lessons in life? I ask people about their own experiences when it comes to the paranormal. Have they ever seen a ghost? Have they had premonitions or knowings? Have they ever ignored their premonitions or knowings? Or trusted them? How did things work out for them? I ask them to tell me about their dreams and their beliefs around Guides and Angels.

Everyone has a story to tell and telling them raises the vibration and energy in the room, in preparation for their Reading. I like to then tell people the following information about what my Team have taught me;

Just like I am sitting on this chair, holding this cup, I know that Souls are just as real. I work with your Soul in the here and now. In this lifetime.

Soul Slippers

We have all come into this lifetime to continue our learning at a higher level. During our lifetime as a human, we start our educational journey in kindergarten then move up through the primary school levels and onto high school. We may decide at this point that we would like to or need to learn more or we may decide that it's time to take what we've learnt and apply it in our lives so that we can earn an income or perhaps teach people what we've come to learn.

Education takes many years. Many lessons. Many tests and a whole lot of patience and homework. Educating the Soul takes time. Lifetimes.

Whilst on a human level we all choose to learn different things in life academically, as Souls, all our lessons are esoteric, not academic. Our Souls know exactly what we need to learn in this life time. It delivers us into a family where by we can learn those lessons; or maybe teach the lessons.

Everyone comes into this lifetime at different levels spiritually. Some of our Souls are learning lessons at kindergarten level whilst others are learning them at high school or university level. This explains too why we get frustrated with others around us. But when we look at the very things that frustrate us about others in our lives and then look internally to ourselves, we see that the very qualities that frustrate us are innate within us and therefore ours to teach, by example.

This is not about the ego saying I'm better than you are, it's about our Soul knowing its journey. Some people live in their Souls 50 to 60% of the time. Others, 90% of the time. Others again 2 to 5% of the time. This is why we clash. This clash is what alerts us that we are in each other's lives to either teach or learn from each other.

It's frustrating for a university student to teach a kindergarten child about complicated subjects. But if the university student is smart, they recognise that they only need teach the child the basics of the topic to begin with, not the whole thing. How to tie up shoelaces leads to an understanding of physics. ABC's lead to an understanding of complicated grammar. To teach at the level required by that person's Soul is divine.

The wisdom carried by the Soul at university level, is to know that they are here to teach at the level required by the student. Not at the level already acquired by the teacher.

So, when next you clash with someone in your life, step out of your human shoes and slip on your Soul Slippers. Everything will then become clearer. Everyone is in your life for a reason, it's best you find out what.

SOUL FOOD

The Big Why?

"I spend a lot of my time thinking about the hereafter these days. I walk into a room and then wonder, what am I hereafter?"

Why am I here? Many people struggle with this question. What is my purpose? Simply, you are your purpose.

People usually ask these types of questions when they have lost their way from or just begun their spiritual journey. They're all reasonable questions. When we open up to seeking more meaning in life, we understand more fully that we have a real purpose for being here.

But your purpose isn't as complicated as you might imagine. It's quite simple really. Our minds complicate our purpose far more than is necessary.

Your purpose is to find you, the real you. Sounds simple, right? But the process is complex and can often take ninety plus years to unravel. Then and only then can you kick back in your rocking chair, look back, and very clearly see everything that brought you to that point.

You were born to have experiences. That's very important to understand. You were born to explore life itself and to gain a deeper understanding of existence. How deep you go depends on the decisions you make in life. You can be anything you choose. It is just a decision away.

Usually a personal crisis brings us to the point of spiritual awakening. Once we've pushed through the hard times and the pain, we receive the epiphany of understanding.

CAUGHT BETWEEN TWO WORLDS

The why. Initially, you may feel that all you want to do is share that epiphany. However, I caution you. That new understanding is specific to you and your journey. So if you're going to share it, be ready for people to not accept it.

Everyone will have his or her own wakeup call in his or her own way. We must balance our lives. When we gain insight, feel gratitude, or are blessed by experience, we want others to experience the same because we know how awesome it feels. It's then that it's prudent to remember that some people are still in spiritual high school. We feel like we've graduated from spiritual university. But they need to graduate the stage they're in before they receive an invitation to learn more. So if and when you share where you're at, make sure you know where they're at. It will avoid unnecessary tension.

Regardless of how you choose to live your life, only you know the ingredients for a recipe of love, laughter and happy memories in your life. There is no need to justify yourself to the world by helping everyone at your own expense.

It's a mistake easily made. We feel grateful and appreciate the life we have been given and we feel that we need to repay the universe. We do this because we want others to experience what we do. We say yes when we mean no. We become people pleasers. Our motivation is coming from the right place, but it was never meant to feel this difficult. We are of no use to others if we have run ourselves into the ground. So put yourself back at the top of your triangle.

SOUL FOOD

Always remember that we all receive our wakeup call when it is the right time for us. Not a second before or after. If you try to give someone a hand up when they are not ready, they will only fall and you will be disappointed. Just like school, we progress from kindergarten up through primary school then high school and then either to college or university or we enter the work force. Either way, we can only do so at the perfect time. Not before and not after. Life is orchestrated perfectly. If only we could accept that, it would flow so much smoother.

Your Book of Life has sequential chapters for a reason. They follow in logical succession. New characters are introduced with each chapter. The story line ebbs and flows. The drama increases and subsides. Sometimes the suspense is too much. Sometimes Groundhog Day bores us to tears. But still, it's an unbelievable read.

Many people struggle with trying to find their soul's purpose in this life because they are too busy running away from it. Consciously or unconsciously, they do what they can for others and forsake themselves. We think this is a very gracious thing to do. But in fact, we only miss the special person we are because we are too busy giving them to everyone else. As hard as it is for some, putting yourself first is of paramount importance.

I have recently embarked on my own journey on my own and I am scared as hell. Not scared of the dark, scared of myself. Will I like myself or will I try to run? I have always valued myself by how much I did for others. I have always avoided myself. If we live true to ourselves and give to ourselves first, we actually shine much brighter. We attract others to us as they see our glow and want to know what's going on. They've noticed a difference. Like a ripple effect, everyone around us benefits from our balanced and effervescent attitude. They then in turn infect others with the same joy. This, surely, is good work.

We don't realise it at the time, but when we do too much for others, they often feel obligated to pay us back. In fact, they can then feel responsible for our happiness and self-worth. Think about this for a minute. What if they don't like something you do for them? Should they pretend to like it just so they don't hurt your feelings? Food for thought.

There is no wrong choice when it comes to discovering your purpose in this life. Because you are the purpose. Your primary purpose – one that is difficult for many to achieve – is to live authentically. To develop the courage and inner strength to be who you are – not who others think you should be or want you to be.

In life we tend to get hung up on the conditioning from societal norms, family and cultural belief systems. We become fixed in these ways of thinking and start to let go of our sense of self. Have you ever wondered why people adore babies? It's because of their potential – they haven't been jaded by life yet. They are completely open and willing to absorb all the different experiences around them. We revere babies and young children because we long to be like them ourselves – to be able to explore and have freedom to learn and grow.

Your Soul's purpose is to live as a child – even in your adult world of responsibilities and obligations. You need to take time to live authentically, to be who you are – or your soul loses its sense of purpose and you struggle to find a sense of meaning.

The Casting Call

There simply is no other way for our Soul to learn its lessons. It must incarnate into a body for a period of time so that the pre-determined lessons can be experienced. The Soul knows it has a specific intention or purpose that needs to be achieved in that lifetime.

Our soul knows what we need to learn from our life. We just need to turn up to our casting call when it's our turn to go on stage. We meander our way through our script much as an actor does. Sometimes, we feel we have to wait years for our turn to go on stage. We cannot go on stage before our time. We must wait for the exact cue.

You see, it's not just our lives that need to be in alignment. It's also that of the other characters in our play. They are navigating their way through their own plots. Their plots will bring them to the right time and the right place to be joined by you in their Play. The two stories then become one.

During our years of waiting for our role, we may become disillusioned or impatient. We may feel like we are wasting precious time rather than realising that this period of time is actually perfect and necessary as a way of strengthening our Soul. This waiting period is a test in itself. We must wait till everyone is in place in their own lives in order to undertake their role in our lives. This cannot be done before they are ready.

We can use this waiting time to our benefit. We can align our thoughts and feelings with our Soul. Bringing them into our conscious self to prepare us for our growth, change and purpose. Making us stronger.

Looking for your Soul Mate? Look within

Am I someone's Soul Mate? You should be your own Soul Mate first and foremost. Until you are, you cannot be a Soul Mate to another person and another person cannot be yours. It's unreasonable to expect that you can find a Soul Mate until you are ready to receive them.

Your Soul Mate will be attracted to you when the time is right, often when you least expect it. When you've been busy learning and growing and getting on with life, a Soul Mate will come into your life; when you are ready and have done the work on yourself that is necessary to be able to share your life with another. This, of course, doesn't mean that you won't have to sift through some who aren't your soul mate first. When a relationship fails, take it as a sign that the work within yourself is not complete. Don't project it on them.

A Soul Mate is not there to learn your lessons for you. A Soul Mate is not there to complete you. A Soul Mate is there to compliment you and to share your life with you. During our lives, we make decisions. These all lead to us meeting our Soul Mate, who, like us, has been making decisions in their own lives.

The idea of the soul mate has shown up in nearly every culture on the globe throughout history. It has consistently been linked to the concept of destiny. In East Asia, there is a legend called the red thread of destiny in which a mystical red string is tied to the fingertips of two meant-to-be lovers. Although the string can twist, turn, and bend, this bond will ultimately ensure their destined meeting.

We meet our destined love by doing what we love. This is because the journey to our beloved, or our destiny, is actually a journey inward. We meet our destined love by being ourselves and doing what we do anyway. Destined loves are not always destined to last. Destiny simply means what you are meant to do. Nowhere does destiny ever claim to be endlessly positive. We've all got struggles that we're destined for, that's part of Karma. Just because a relationship doesn't work out doesn't mean it wasn't destined for you to meet that person and vice versa.

When we encounter a Soul Mate, or someone with whom we feel we have a Spiritual or Soul connection, they come along in order to represent a choice. Soul Mates appear in our lives to open up new doors, new possibilities for our future, and show us that there is a fork in the road. Our souls make pacts with one another before we're born. They decide that our paths will cross in order to help each other grow and develop spiritually. In this way, each of our destined loves have played a role in propelling us forward on our spiritual paths in some way.

This idea might be difficult for some to swallow. Suggesting that even the abusive and sometimes violent relationships are based on soul contracts is unpopular. But I urge you to reflect on your life and think about what you've learnt from the relationships you've had. Then tell me honestly that a single one of them didn't enter your life to present you an opportunity for growth.

Remember, it's all about choices. Anyone who has ever empowered themselves enough to leave an abusive relationship can tell you that the choice to do so was not a step, but rather a giant leap in their spiritual evolution. This is also why it is important to allow yourself time to heal between relationships, and not jump into a new one right away.

By spending some time reviewing the issues that came up in you, and being truly honest with yourself about why it failed, you can honour this soul contract process and really do some work on yourself. If you don't take the time to do this, you'll inadvertently take all of your baggage with you into your next relationship.

You will then most likely need to engage the help of Psychologists or Counsellors, who I refer to as baggage handlers, to help you get your life back in order. Otherwise, you'll find yourself dealing with the same issues in one relationship after another.

When you take the time to do this type of inner work, and spend time contemplating and becoming more self-aware of your issues surrounding relationships, you will heal and subsequently begin to vibrate energetically at a higher level. Because a destined soul mate is someone whose level of vibration matches your own, you will eventually attract your Soul Mate.

The more we heal and learn about ourselves through the work of being in a relationship with another person, the better quality relationship we will be capable of. Moreover, remember, your destined love is also doing this inner work and is hoping that their destined path will lead them to you.

If you have not yet met your Soul Mate, don't feel despair. They are just not ready yet. Take comfort that they are still learning their lessons so that they can be the best 'mate' they can be for you. This is, after all, what you want.

What we need to remember here is to keep the focus on ourselves, as the journey to your beloved, or your destined love, is ultimately a journey to yourself.

Religion will generally always discourage inward focus. I recommend it. Keeping your focus directed inward creates power within yourself. When you can do that, you will have a real magnetism that will attract all of the right people and circumstances into your life. You create your own destiny by following your own path, and your destined soul mate lies along that path.

What we are looking for is not our match, but rather our complement. Like trying to use two forks to eat dinner. They match each other, and you'll have some success. But ultimately if you use a knife and fork instead, they'll complement each other and work together more efficiently. You're not looking for another you, you're looking for the soul that complements you so you can get stuff done in life.

Looking for someone to complete you gives your potential mate the balance of power. Believing that you're incomplete without a partner is dangerous. Because you aren't. You don't need another soul to make you whole, but you do need them to help you grow. So searching for your 'other half' attracts a partner who may exploit and abuse the natural imbalance of power. You are a whole person on your own, and you want to attract someone else who is whole as well. In this way, your next relationship will avoid the drama and pain that your previous ones may have caused.

We take the time and effort to be incarnated in human form so that we can learn, and life is truly a school filled with lessons of various types. The most important lesson we are confronted with during our experiences over many lifetimes involves love. Quite simply, love is why we exist. On all levels.

If you are not currently in a relationship, then it is important to examine that as well. Are you still healing from the last one? Do you still feel anger, bitterness, and resentment toward any of your previous partners? Are you afraid? Or, are you being confronted with the lesson of being patient and waiting for the right person to cross paths with you? Taking note of this, and becoming aware of where you are at regarding relationship issues is a vital step toward uncovering your destiny and bringing you closer to being ready for a Soul Mate in your life. It's not a reason to be critical of yourself, simply a chance to reflect objectively.

Find out more about who you really are, do what you love, and discover the places that you enjoy. Don't stop living your life. Sitting home and hoping you will meet your Soul Mate won't achieve anything. Keep your focus on yourself, create your own power, and walk your life's path with your heart and your eyes open, because somewhere on the road ahead you will encounter your love, waiting in exactly the right spot. It's your destiny.

A Love That's Destined

Destiny! One of the most romantic notions we can possibly attach to the concept of love. That you will meet someone, and right away. That you will both know that you were just meant to be.

Not overtly practical, is it? It's also not the experience of the majority of the population. And when they think about the concept of a love that's destined for them, the questions start to flow. Are we destined to meet a Soul Mate? Does that mean that it is all predetermined and therefore we don't have a choice? How does destiny work when it comes to love then?

Let's first define what destiny is. In order to do that, we need to accept that destiny is the understanding and belief that the universe has a natural order. One that we don't define but can positively or negatively influence. It's as sure as night follows day and summer follows spring. There is something greater than us. If you can appreciate this concept, then you can appreciate, and maybe even begin to comprehend, destiny.

An important thing to understand first, is that a Soul knows its own destiny. A mind does not. The soul knows the way, the mind is lost. Lock that away.

Now, think on this: predestined and predetermined are not the same thing. Our lives are predestined, but they are not predetermined. Predestination allows for choices to be made. Choices for which the Soul knows right option. Destiny is something that we actively participate in. We can choose our destiny.

So, how does this relate to love? Do we get to choose our destined love? Well, we have many soul mates of different types and meeting them is predestined. Some we meet because we have karma to work out. Others we meet so we can learn lessons about giving and receiving love. Each and every one of these soul mates is our part of our predestined path. A path that the soul knows the map for like the back of its hand.

Your soul mate could be described as someone with whom you have an instant connection. Sometimes, that connection develops over years. Either way, you just seem to know when you have found this person. That knowing feeling, that's your soul. Your connection to this person will feel irresistibly strong. You will feel love as if you've never ever felt it before. The longer you're with this person, the deeper your connection intertwines.

This person loves you unconditionally and vice versa. They'd do anything for you and vice versa. They know you instinctively and vice versa. You feel as if you have known this person all your life, even if you have just met them. All these signs are your soul communicating with your mind, letting it know that the right decision here is to stay with this person in front of the body's eyes.

When you have met a Soul Mate you will just know that they were worth waiting for. A Soul Mate allows you to be you, loves you for you, encourages you to be you and does not try to change you. You feel like you have finally come home. That's because your soul has been on a journey to this point.

But not all Soul Mates are destined to be with us forever. Meeting them is predestined, choosing to learn from them is our choice. And meeting them can be messy. Whilst it would be nice to experience all the emotions in the previous paragraph immediately, it doesn't always happen that way. We may not be attracted to a potential soul mate in the beginning. We may actually clash with them. All relationships take time, whether they start with a bang or puff.

Our soul mates will help us learn the tough lessons in life and then afterwards may disappear from our lives altogether. This can happen, but it doesn't mean they weren't meant to be part of our lives. Being left to figure out what the lesson was can be painful, but it's important work.

CAUGHT BETWEEN TWO WORLDS

People fear they have only one romantic soul mate available to them in their life. This is a myth. Just think how it would be if you met this special someone only to lose them! That would be inconceivable, wouldn't it? Some religions might like you to believe that God is that cruel, but I can assure you the universe is not! If you thought there was only one soul mate for you and things started to go wrong, you would try everything to hang onto them even when it was not working for either of you anymore. You would be scared to let go wouldn't you? And then how would you learn anything…?

Each partner brings with them love and lessons. They're all there to help you love and teach.

Life's Little Secrets

Life's Directory – Using your PPS

We've all heard of a GPS – Global Positioning System. Well, we have a PPS too, a Personal Positioning System. How many times have you blamed the GPS for not taking the road that you wanted to drive down? I can see you now yelling at it because it missed the road you perceived to have been the right road to take you to where you wanted to go?

Life is a little like that at times.

It is so much easier to blame something else than take responsibility for ourselves when our lives do not seem to be working out as we would like. This is where we resort to, refer to, rely on or put faith in Fate, Destiny, Serendipity, Synchronicity and hope that the planets are aligning. Boy, there's a lot of ifs, buts and maybes in that lot.

Yet, if you use your PPS to look out for Life's Signposts, you'll get along much better. Sure, there are intersections and sometimes the directions are cryptic. But hey, that's life.

Is there such a thing as a wrong turn in life? No! Your life is like a street directory, it has many roads but they all lead somewhere. Your destiny has been pre-orchestrated and your PPS is your tool for navigating it.

See your life as a play – it has a beginning, an end, a plot, actors, characters, scenes, surprise twists, happiness and sadness. Some of the scenes are boring, some are funny, and some are full of surprises (including romance). Not every scene contains every one of these things, even though we'd like it that way most of the time. If they were to happen in every scene of our life, they would no longer be special.

Every story has an author. You may think your life has been pre-orchestrated, but the conductor is nowhere to be seen. We have to trust in the story that has been written especially for us. There are times when we come to crossroads. Decisions need to be made and our life, for a short time anyway, may be unsettled. This is where a Psychic can help you decide which road to take - by looking further down the road, further than you can see yourself.

A GPS will take you the most direct route from point A to point B, using a mapped system of roads and highway. Sure, you will get there in a shorter time but what will you miss out on the way? A GPS can only provide well-known routes and sometimes we find out the hard way that it will take you the wrong way; losing precious time and creating angst and frustration.

By using your PPS, we can explore all the other options available to you that may be more interesting, varied and exciting. Your destination will be the same; it is just the journey that will be different. A psychic Reading may actually offer you a shortcut rather than wasting valuable time exploring unnecessary paths to your destination.

The choice is always yours, but consider giving yourself some more options. Wouldn't it help sometimes if someone could tell you the difference between all the choices? And guide you toward which choice to make?

Fate

Oh how we love that word, handing ourselves over to it when something nice happens to us but ignoring it when things don't go our way. Fate, in the end, is about staying on purpose.

I've had many things happen in my life that are too amazing for mere coincidence. I'd hope the readings in this book are proof of that. I believe fate is a tool of God, designed to help us fulfil our destiny and work out our karma.

Many of the stories at the beginning of my book are a result of fate. Situations are put in our path with purpose. It's up to us if we take that opportunity or not. I guess fate could be considered Divine Intervention. Life actually flows a lot easier and smoother when we trust in Fate.

However, we still have the free will to go with it or not. Fate is the force that puts you in a particular place at a particular time to help with your soul's evolution. Sometimes it is a painful, hard lesson to be learned and sometimes it is positive and joyous. Either way you grow.

The answers vary from Psychic to Psychic, school to school, but there are some common themes. We live in the midst of a Divine Paradox. We have free will and Karma, Fate, and Destiny each may play a role in our lives at one time or another… Still, it is up to us how we handle it.

Karma

You've no doubt heard this word bandied about. Question is, what does it mean for you? Does it even apply to you? The answer to that last question is always a resounding yes. No one is untouched by karma.

Everything you think, feel, act, say or do has its own energy. It is real. It all has an effect on others and, consequently, the universe. Everything has a consequence. Consequence is a huge part of karma. You cannot just say or do hurtful things to others and expect to get away with it. Those you hurt may not be the ones to hurt you back but the universe has a scoreboard. Someone, somewhere, somehow will pay you back.

Karma relates to anything you do – positive or negative. Nevertheless, be aware that it is much better for you to put out positive vibes than negative ones. After all, what do you want to have come back to you? That, after all, is the real choice here.

The Universe keeps a karmic scoreboard. Every time you do something spiritually loving, you get runs on the positive side of the scoreboard. Every time you do something spiritually negative, you get runs on the negative side of the scoreboard. Karma will come back to you in this lifetime. Choose your Karma carefully.

Living spiritually is based on the law of karmic awareness. The Spiritual Law of Karma has been around for longer than any of the religions that use it as a basis. It takes a conscious effort and at times, you will forget. You may judge others or may hurt others unintentionally as a reaction to the hurt you felt inflicted by them initially. You may act out of impulse and/or retaliation. Question your motivation here. Why did you do this? Not only have you hurt them but you have also hurt yourself because now you have created an affect that will come back to you.

Sometimes we hurt others with our words in order to make ourselves feel more confident within. The fact that we cannot understand that our actions are hurtful doesn't change how painful they are for those that we're hurting. Funny though, how when we do something nice for someone else without them expecting it, that actually makes us feel good about ourselves for doing it.

Feel the difference? This is the perfect time to realise that spiritually, we all have lessons to learn. We cannot all be goody goodies all the time – that's impossible, and boring. We are, after all, human beings learning to be spiritual beings.

Always be aware of what you do to others though. What you say, what you think and the actions you take all have consequences.

CAUGHT BETWEEN TWO WORLDS

Karma can be expressed as the law of moral cause and effect. If only more people understood how karma works, surely we'd all choose to put out good karma. Why would we want crap to come back to us? So if you feel like you're tired of life dealing you up shit, think about what you're putting out.

If you're brave enough, do an experiment. I don't recommend doing something bad to someone else. I do, however, recommend doing something nice with no expectation of a return/reward. Keep a watch out over the next few weeks – the opportunity to help a stranger will arise – take the opportunity to create good karma. Then when you least expect it and you need help right when you do not have help – a stranger will help you.

Watch your thoughts, your actions and especially your judgement of others. This is particularly true if you are finding it hard to make friends or feel left out at work. Look at it this way – you are teaching others how you want to be treated yourself. If you come across as friendly, helpful, caring, compassionate and empathetic, so will others be with you.

If you come across as selfish, hostile, impolite and impatient, you're teaching people this is your preferred way to be treated in return. Take the time to stop and put yourself in their shoes. Look into their eyes and feel the situation from where they stand. Feel the pain you are inflicting. Hopefully, it will make you think again.

I know which action I would choose. Mind you, I only started choosing positive karma once I had learned the consequences the hard way. I still don't always get it right. These days, the universe is speeding up its repayment of karma. It used to take place over generations and reincarnations. Now, many people are experiencing a working out of their karma in this very lifetime.

The other day, I was backing out of a car park and wanted to beat a lady who was also backing out of a car park further up the row. I wanted to get in front of her and cut her off so that I could get home quickly. I was craning my neck to get a good look at her. In doing so, I hit the car parked in the bay opposite me. I got my karma back instantly. I then had to get out of the car and deal with the incident while the other woman, oblivious to my motivations was able to drive out of the shopping centre car park way before I could. She had done no wrong – but I had and was instantly repaid. I guess that debt is cleared now, I hope.

How good do you feel when you perform a random act of kindness? It's great isn't it? It makes you feel all warm inside, knowing you have helped someone in genuine need. Now consider that you have created a positive score on the karma scoreboard. It should encourage you to perform more random acts of kindness, because you are creating positive karma for yourself.

At our local supermarket, they sell flowers. When doing my regular shop, I always buy flowers for myself. I also buy a bunch to give away at the mall while I'm there.

I remember one occasion two years ago. I saw an older woman looking terribly sad. I went up to speak with her. I told her that I would like to give her the bunch of flowers as I thought it might make her day. Initially she was hesitant but when I told her I do this regularly, her eyes welled up with tears as she reached out for the flowers and said to me, "Thank you so much. I had a best friend for 30 years and I haven't heard from her for a while. She walked past me just 10 minutes ago, looked me in the eye and didn't acknowledge me. I feel so sad and I don't know what I've done wrong. These flowers are very timely. Thank you."

I don't give away bunches of flowers to put scores on the karmic scoreboard. I do so because I love the joy it brings and hopefully to take some scores off the negative side of my scoreboard. Nonetheless, it gives me great pleasure to give them.

Don't make all your acts conscious scores on the karma scoreboard. Just make your motivation clean. At the end of each day, check in with your conscience. Did you rip anyone off today? Did you make a coffee for anyone today? Did you cut someone off in traffic today? Did you smile for anyone or hold the door open to let someone through today? Did you offer a helping hand today? Were you deliberately nasty or hurtful today? Did you play mind games or emotionally blackmail anyone today in order to get something you wanted? These will all come back to you regardless of whether you believe in it or not.

According to the law of Karma, all suffering experienced is deserved. Mostly this comes from past lives. In summary, bad deeds committed in past lives must be paid for and this would explain why bad things happen to good people – they are paying for deeds from their past lives. It's the only way it can make sense. Karma is pretty simple. Give out what you want to receive back.

I like to focus on this life. After all, it's the one we are living now and is tangible to us now. It's the only one we have control over. If you bring your awareness to all you do each day, you will soon see karma at work in its own way. Watch the acts of others, especially those who are constantly going through hard times. What is it they are putting out/doing to others? Can they go to bed at night and say they have a clean conscience?

You can't change what others do, but you can change what you do. It is my belief that the more good and wonderful karma you create for yourselves in this life, the more you'll learn in this life – bringing you closer to the end goal and reducing the need to reincarnate.

You have no control over how other people treat you – that is their karma to work through. You have a choice as to how you will react though – and that is your karma.

Karma therefore, is a choice. A conscious choice. If you would like to enjoy a happy, peaceful and love filled life – then live that way, consciously! Live it for yourself, for your family, your colleagues your friends and anyone you come across. It is much easier to live this way. Even just giving a smile to a stranger creates good karma! You will enjoy pleasing others with your actions and you can look forward to the great karma coming back to you. Give and you shall receive.

If you 'choose' to remain selfish, deliberately hostile,

jealous, judgemental, negative and even hurtful towards others – these choices will leave you very unhappy searching for happiness. Trust me, you'll hate it. Make your choices wisely – after all, you really are the only one who can make them for you! Realise that we are all here on different spiritual levels to learn different lessons to the next person. It is our journey.

By now you've probably examined your conscience, behaviour patterns and actions to find that some of the above rings true for you. You may tell yourself you'd really like to make a change for the better. But, you do not know where to start to create good karma. Well, here is some pointers that I use:

+ Smile at anyone and everyone
+ Love unconditionally
+ Be kind
+ Be respectful
+ Be a good listener
+ Always have a clean conscience in all you do
+ Don't judge others – they have their own karma they're dealing with
+ Be aware of what you think, do or say – try and be

positive

+ If you are negative at times, give yourself a second chance and learn from the lesson

+ Make the time to be human being not a human doing

+ Look at your life – Be grateful for it and all you have in it

+ Don't be materialistic

+ Enjoy the little things in life

+ Stop rushing about – you just don't know what you might have missed

+ Be prepared for others to teach you – you don't know everything after all

+ Most importantly: just try to be nice. That is, after all, what you would like to have back.

Yesterday when I went walking, I smiled at a woman who just walked straight past me and looked through me. Today when I passed her, she smiled back! Maybe tomorrow, she will pass on her own smile.

Synchronicity

You know, that feeling of being in the right place at the right time, usually only obvious in hindsight. The universe synchronises time, people and situations for the best outcome in your life.

Synchronicity is the special moment in which destiny summons us to move forward. It is the spur of the moment that initiates growth. This is the process by which archetypal reality incarnates itself in historical time.

Synchronicity is the strikingly meaningful coincidence of two events or of a series of events. It can also be the coincidence of a psychic perception and a simultaneously occurring event, as happens in ESP. Premonitions are in this category. In both ESP and premonition, the case can be made for synchronicity if meaningfulness is present. Meaningfulness is always the ultimate criterion of synchronicity.

Synchronicity appears in our work on ourselves. There may be synchronicity in the fact that our knowledge of our shortcomings, in ourselves and in our relationships, comes simultaneously with the strength to change them. We are usually in denial for a long time before we finally recognize and acknowledge the truth about ourselves.

When we are ready to learn, a teacher appears. This is synchronicity. Occasionally a person passed over comes to mind repeatedly in the course of a week or more. It could be that the meaning of that person in our life is coming home to us in a compelling way. Perhaps we learned something from that person and need to remember it now. Perhaps there is something we are now ready to learn. This may be another form of synchronicity. The face of the teacher appears when the time has come to be instructed or to gain a deeper insight into who we are. This might even be the time to ask that person to be our guide from the other world if that fits our worldview.

Synchronicity also occurs in looking back on your life and seeing how it all prepared you for the fullest fruition of your potential. A hidden feeling or truth waited to be awakened by just the right person or circumstance, sometimes painfully. My destiny had to have just such a beginning. My neglectful father helped me practice for the independent life I live now. My empty cupboard helped me care about starving children.

Sensitive People (Empaths)

Did you know that about 15-20% of the population is considered highly sensitive? It's such a significant part of the population that it cannot be considered a condition, and the numbers are not large enough to make it common, so it's not quite understood.

Many people look at being sensitive as a defect or a hindrance because it does not fit into societal norms of how one should act in public. On the contrary, sensitive people are more aware, more compassionate, more forgiving and often more driven.

Sensitive people believe things can be better and work hard to make it so. It is hard for a sensitive person to see suffering without trying to relieve the pain, to see heartache without expressing love and to see a challenge without problem solving. The empathetic nature of a sensitive person is often invisible to most, and as such, is often ignored or misunderstood.

Sensitive people are often so giving of their time and energy that they forget to care for themselves. An innate quality can be difficult to navigate with outside influences establishing the expectations of how you should act.

If you feel like this might be you, here are 5 important lessons for sensitive people:

1. Embrace and control your emotional responses.

Sensitive people see the world differently and with that vision comes great power and responsibility. Because we feel what others are feeling, we often feel a moral obligation to help, and we react with bigger emotion and more rapid action. On the surface, this appears to be a good thing, an admirable trait.

There are many challenges with reacting to a situation in the heat of heightened emotion. The other person might not want help, we might not be able to provide the right kind of help or we might offer help that ends up doing more harm than good to them and us.

It is not about the desire to help; it is about understanding the true nature of any situation outside of the emotional connection that is felt. Take the time to think both logically and emotionally before jumping into action. Know the whole world cannot be saved no matter how hard we try. The responsibility comes in choosing our reactions wisely.

LIFE'S LITTLE SECRETS

2. Listen and trust your inner guide to protect yourself.

Sensitive people have a strong intuition that comes from a heightened awareness of what is happening around us. Unfortunately, though, we do not always pay attention to what our gut is telling us.

Because of our highly sensitive nature, we tend to be more trusting and more willing to take people at their word. There are people that will take advantage of that, and that is why listening to our inner guide is so important.

It is this inner source of wisdom that protects us and warns us to tread carefully. As sensitive people, we are so focused on helping that we often ignore the warning signs our inner guide provides. Pay attention to your gut as closely as you pay attention to your desire to help others. Doing so will help you help yourself which better positions you to help others.

3. Stay focused on the things that really matter.

Because we are so aware and absorb so much of the energy that surrounds us, it is easy to lose our focus and take on other people's problems as if they are our own. It is important that we stay focused on the things that matter in our lives first and avoid over-committing ourselves to the point of being overwhelmed.

We are quick to say yes but upon contemplation might realize we are not be the best person for the task. This can lead to over-complicating and overthinking a situation to the point that it becomes detrimental to our responsibilities. The lesson here is to keep our priorities first, help when it makes sense and find other resources when necessary.

4. Being sensitive is not the same as being weak.

People who are not as sensitive as we are may interpret our ability to empathize and feel as a weakness. The truth is, it takes great inner strength to feel the constant joy, sadness and even heartache of those around us. This is not a burden we choose to carry but a gift with which we were entrusted.

The key to using our gift with purpose, and in service to others, is to rely on that inner strength. That strength helps us to stay strong and keep from internalizing the energy that is so easy for us to absorb. It gives us the fortitude to use the energy we encounter and repurpose it back into the universe with grace and positivity.

5. Be courageous and continue to live from your authentic truth.

The biggest lesson for sensitive people is to not let others, who might not understand our gift, change us. It is often easier to hide our sensitive side than to be judged by it. Continue to live your truth and be proud of your sensitive nature. It is who we are, and the Universe needs us to share it. Doing so will create a more loving, kind and peaceful world.

LIFE'S LITTLE SECRETS

Always remember being sensitive is a gift and even the greatest gifts can be a burden at times. Remember these lessons to keep yourself grounded in your true nature while honouring yourself and those your gift serves.

www.ingramcontent.com/pod-product-compliance
Lightning Source LLC
Chambersburg PA
CBHW051939290426
44110CB00015B/2042